"Barbara eloquently tells the story of her sudden tragic stroke at a very young age . . . She offers hope and encouragement to others by stressing the three P's of stroke recovery, Patience, Positive Attitude and Perseverance."

> Thelma Edwards R.N. National Stroke Association

"This book is about courage and healing. It pushes the boundaries of the human spirit. *Return to Ithaca* will make you proud to be a human being."

> Larry Dossey, M.D. author of *Prayer is Good Medicine,*
> *Healing Words, Meaning and Medicine* and *Recovering the Soul*
> and also the Executive editor of *Alternative Therapies*

"an inspirational triumph over adversity . . . a good read."

> Joseph Jaffe M.D.

"The world is better for the presence of this writing. One more light to show the way home."

> Emmanuel communicated through Pat Rodegast,
> author of the bestselling Emmanuel books

". . . no book has shown so clearly what a soul-shattering experience it is, and what a traumatic journey has to be taken to reach a place where life is bearable and fruitful."

> Valerie Eaton Griffith M.B.E., founder: Dysphasic support
> The Stroke Association

"This book is not tragedy, it is about struggle, perseverance and love. It is about a journey to one's true self . . . Barbara has given birth to herself while awakening to life's adventures. It is no coincidence her name is Barbara Newborn."

> Bernie Siegel M.D., author of *Love, Medicine and Miracles*

RETURN TO ITHACA

Barbara Newborn is Chief of Staff at the National Stroke and Quality of Life Medical Education Institute, a division of the American Institute of Life-Threatening Illness and Loss based at Columbia Presbytarian Medical Center. In addition she is a qualified rehabilitation counselor for families and the survivors of strokes in New York City. A pioneer of rehabilitation programs for those affected by disability, she works enthusiastically to raise disability awareness among healthcare professionals and among the general public.

Return to Ithaca

A Woman's Triumph Over the Disabilities of a Severe Stroke

BARBARA NEWBORN

[handwritten inscription:]

1-3/02

Carl
— May our friendship
grow and share the
wisdom from eachother!
with love & laughter
Barbay

ELEMENT

Shaftesbury, Dorset • Rockport, Massachusetts
Brisbane, Queensland

© Element Books Limited 1997
text © Barbara Newborn 1997

First published in Great Britain in 1997 by
Element Books Limited
Shaftesbury, Dorset SP7 8BP

Published in the USA in 1997 by
Element Books, Inc.
PO Box 830, Rockport, MA 01966

Published in Australia in 1997 by
Element Books Limited
for Jacaranda Wiley Limited
33 Park Road, Milton, Brisbane 4064

Cover design by Max Fairbrother
Design and typeset by Footnote Graphics, Warminster, Wiltshire
Printed and bound in Great Britain by
Creative Print and Design Group (Wales), Ebbw Vale

British Library Cataloguing in Publication
data available

Library of Congress Cataloging in Publication
data available

ISBN 1-85230-944-X

Contents

Acknowledgements

I wish to thank Irene and Roy Newborn, my wonderful parents, who supported me all the way in this expedition and gave me everything that I have and am. My special thanks to: John Baldock, who was with me all the way from conception to final print, encouraging and guiding me with his words of wisdom; Wallace Sife, Ph.D., a treasured friend, skilled editor, word-processing wizard, who devoted countless amounts of time, interest and caring to make this book a reality; Jack Adolfi, who is an inspiration to me, as we worked together harmoniously for many long hours in finalizing the book; Hadi N. Pearlman, who devoted her patience, time and love to the beginning stages of the book; Lori Muskat, whose friendship and sound advice I treasure; and Antonin Nenov, my husband and partner, who reread those endless rewrites with love; and to the many others who helped create this book. Thank you.

I would also like to acknowledge the support and encouragement of the National Stroke and Quality of Life Medical Education Institute (NSEI), a division of the American Institute of Life-Threatening Illness and Loss, in the preparation of this book.

Introduction

Life-threatening illness throws the individual and his or her family into chaos, and dramatically alters and affects their lives. The helplessness and loss of control one feels under such circumstances is profound. One is suddenly placed in a very dependent situation, which affects one's entire social system and everything that was familiar. This is a frightening time for everyone involved, filled with overwhelming unknowns for the future.

In this journey of recovery, we often feel we must hold onto our old selves. We want things to be just the way they were before the tragedy. We are suddenly alone, feeling a terror and a terrible sense of loss. Yet disability teaches us about ourselves, if we listen to our hearts and remain open to ourselves and each other. Living through this crisis, while remaining compassionate, our true inner selves can become known to us. We can develop a new appreciation of our own self and others in a world filled with connections.

This recovery takes tremendous perseverance, courage and faith. The healing process, though slow and painful, often provides a rare opportunity for all individuals to evolve a profound awareness. The situation does not have to remain tragic; a new consciousness can develop instead for everyone who has gone through a life-altering crisis. This tragedy can transform into an adventure journey, where discovery takes place and opens the way to psychological and spiritual growth.

Most of us know of a person we call "remarkable", who is a true survivor of difficult life circumstances. In fact, life's traumas do not impair such a person; rather they provide an opportunity to know him- or herself better. These people not only survive, but evolve from this experience. But they transcend the tragedy by the support of others. Only then can they discover hidden potentials and ways to derive meaning from that event. All it takes is just one person's understanding and compassion to see them as unique, intelligent, feeling human beings.

There is a growing body of knowledge that suggests that negative or positive attitudes have a profound influence on healing. One of the main components is transcending one's role of victim into that of a survivor who regains quality of life. Especially in the case of illness, this recovery may be interrupted or even shut down by anyone whose current beliefs are disempowering. It harms the survivor when others are directed by wrong information or text-book definitions. Their lack of understanding causes them to treat the patient differently, forcing her into a world filled with "cannots", "should nots" and lost hope. The survivor's life is either dismissed or transformed by society's attitudes to illness.

At the age of 21, just graduating from college, I was planning to teach English and speech, and to marry the man of my dreams. Instead, I suffered a severe stroke. Suddenly, I had lost my ability to think and express myself in words, and my body was immobilized. The loss of language devastated me, obliterating my relationship with others and myself. I lost my connection with everything and everyone. In time I would forget myself, because I did not have any words to remind me who I was.

For the first time in my life speech became a conscious and deliberate act, filled with errors, including stuttering, mispronunciations and nonsense words. I became extremely anxious whenever I had to talk to strangers and even good friends; I thought that society now presumed my intelligence to be lessened or even retarded. I could no longer convince anyone that only my speech had been impaired and not myself.

Recovery required a reconstruction of my entire self-image and worth. It was frightening, but I knew I had to adapt to chaotic new situations using a whole new set of rules. My aphasia was not like a broken arm or an attack of appendicitis. Aphasia refers to difficulties one has understanding and using language. This definition, however, does not even hint at the complexity of the psychosocial implications that arise from this disorder. It took my whole being, and a new person had to evolve for healing. At first, my motivation was to regain my old self; I neither wanted to know nor would accept that I was disabled. During these darker moments I was blessed with "angels" who appeared in the form of family, friends, professionals and kind strangers. They freely gave me their support and compassion when my own was impaired. My need to connect with these people was paramount in my healing. No matter what my fears were, I was determined to communicate in any way that I could—with or without speech.

I have written this book as an aphasic. The countless difficulties I've experienced in expressing what I mean in the proper words has caused me to rewrite the text by hand, word by word, line by line, many times over. My right hand is still paralyzed which makes word processing very difficult, so I had to have an assistant help transcribe my verbal dictation. But this book is not just about my own struggles and triumphs, it is also about anyone who has gone through a physical crisis and finds herself alone. An understanding of what the survivor is going through can lead to greater acceptance of our fellow human beings, and of ourselves as well. Basic to all healing is the potential for self-discovery—for finding out who we really are.

This book is intended to provide insights into the turmoil, anguish, triumph and hope in the struggle for healing, but it is not limited to the stroke experience. It will speak to anyone who has faced, or is facing, adversity and loss. It also challenges many of today's traditional definitions of disability and illness, offering new perspectives and showing that personal disability need not be a permanent change for the worse. Disability can teach us about ourselves, bringing into view what is truly important to our personal survival. It enlightens us to observe a new reality in better ways. When forced into an isolated space, one can appreciate one's new self in a new world, making a personal transformation from the external world of appearances into the internal universe of balance, self-worth and faith. After the catastrophic storm there is a rainbow, but one must learn how and where to look for it.

I chose not to be a victim. From my own experience, this word conveys the negative connotation that the person is helpless and passive, and reinforces the belief that illness is only a negative phenomenon. I have become the Spokesperson for the National Stroke and Quality of Life Medical Educational Institute, based in New York City. My function with the NSEI is to raise the consciousness of the public, caregivers, and professionals, by providing information about the psychosocial effects of stroke. This is accomplished by means of seminars, counseling and literature. My planned career, in which language and speech were all-important, was brought to a premature end by my stroke. Yet now, as an author, lecturer, and rehabilitation therapist, I am practicing vocations in which language and speech are all-important. I sometimes feel intimidated by the impressive credentials of professionals compared with my master's degrees in this field. I am often anxious before making presentations to large audiences, thinking I will forget or stumble on a word. But I have to remind myself that I have had more frightening moments in the past, and my wisdom comes from the direct experience of surviving a stroke.

I invite you to retrace the steps of my journey. I hope that sharing the stages of my metamorphosis may be a catalyst in your own exploration. As an old Irish proverb tells us, "It is in the shelter of each other that we live."

Prologue

In my fortieth year, I sat on the banks of an ancient river, near my yoga ashram in Neyer Dam, India. I thought back, calmly and peacefully, on the transformations my life had taken. It all began when I was 21 years old. On my way to Ithaca, New York, to marry my fiancé and begin my career teaching high school English and speech, my dreams were only beginning to take form. But when I arrived in Ithaca, a nightmare took place instead. I was suddenly thrust into a strange and unknown world.

Like Odysseus, I had to struggle to find my way back home, to Ithaca. Both of us had monsters to fight, but of different kinds. And during the treacherous ordeal we each had to keep fixed in our mind the reasons for the journey home. We had to keep our spirits high and fortify the love in our souls. The voyage took many long years, but at last we found gifts of wisdom and joy—riches beyond value.

ITHACA

When you start on your journey to Ithaca,
then pray that the road is long,
full of adventure, full of knowledge.
Do not fear the Lestrygonians
and the Cyclopes and the angry Poseidon.
You will never meet such as these on your path,
if your thoughts remain lofty, if a fine
emotion touches your body and your spirit.
You will never meet the Lestrygonians,
the Cyclopes and the fierce Poseidon,
if you do not carry them within your soul,
if your soul does not raise them up before you.

Then pray that the road is long.
That the summer mornings are many,
that you will enter ports seen for the first time
with such pleasure, with such joy!
Stop at Phoenician markets,
and purchase fine merchandise,
mother-of-pearl and corals, amber and ebony,
and pleasurable perfumes of all kinds,
buy as many pleasurable perfumes as you can;
visit hosts of Egyptian cities,
to learn and learn from those who have knowledge.

Always keep Ithaca fixed in your mind.
To arrive there is your ultimate goal.
But do not hurry the voyage at all.
It is better to let it last for long years;
and even to anchor at the isle when you are old,
rich with all that you have gained on the way,
not expecting that Ithaca will offer you riches.

Ithaca has given you the beautiful voyage.
Without her you would never have taken the road.
But she has nothing more to give you.

And if you find her poor, Ithaca has not defrauded you.
With the great wisdom you have gained, with so much
    experience,
you must surely have understood by then what Ithaca mean.
> (From *The Complete Poems of Cavafy*,
> translated by Rae Dalven)

"It's finally happening," I thought, as I checked in for the night flight from Pittsburgh to Ithaca. No more waiting. I had spent one week in Pennsylvania with my parents, getting a tan in their backyard, and stayed another week visiting family in Long Island. I was now on my way to Ithaca to live with John, my fiancé. My trip to New York had produced three huge suitcases full of living-room drapes, kitchen curtains and yellow flowered bed sheets—all purchased for our first apartment. Having eaten nothing but grapefruit for the past week, I was 10 lbs thinner and could hardly wait to show myself to John.

As I buckled myself into the airplane seat, I began to get nervous so I checked my make-up one more time in a hand mirror. I then put the mirror back into my purse and looked at my watch. I was not just going back to college this time. I would soon be united with the man I would be spending the rest of my life with.

"Excuse me, are you from Ithaca?"

I turned away from the window to see who had asked me the question. A tall, thin man with a kind face wearing horn-rimmed glasses was sitting beside me.

"I will be because I'm going to live with my fiancé in Ithaca," I replied.

"So that's why you look so happy," the stranger stated.

I nodded "Yes," pleased that my delight was so apparent. "I'm beginning a whole new phase of my life."

He, too, was bound for Ithaca. After a ten-year period of medical research in India, he was returning to Cornell University for a college reunion. His gentle voice attracted me, as did his kind and forthright eyes. Yet more than this, I was impressed by his sincerity and warmth. He had done something purposeful with his life while I, at 21, was just beginning to give meaning to my own. I told him that I had just graduated from Ithaca College, which would allow me to teach speech, drama and English in the fall at a nearby junior high school. I then told him how confident I felt about teaching because my speech professors called me a "natural". He nodded affirmingly as I spoke. Then he told me about his life in India, his wife, his work, his child. Pulling a wallet out of his jacket pocket, he produced a photograph of his son, a child of five who had a bright, open smile very much like that of his father.

"He's beautiful," I said, admiring the child's big, bright eyes.

"He's perfect," the doctor murmured, "even though he has cerebral palsy."

I was visibly shocked. "It's hard to tell from the picture," I added, hoping to soften the knee-jerk response to this information. "Was he born this way?" I asked.

"Yes." The doctor's expression turned subtly reflective. "India is a strange country. It is difficult to assimilate the peculiar attitudes the people there have toward life. One of their customs is that when a child is born imperfect it is sometimes rejected at birth and killed."

"What do you mean?" I said rather alarmed. "Who sets the standard for what is and isn't perfect? What right does society have to prejudge innocent people?"

The doctor whispered almost to himself, "They're scared of anyone different—whether one is ill or deformed really doesn't much matter. Society shuns that person, ignoring their feelings and what is inside their soul. Many times a person who is disabled takes on the image that others create for him. He thinks that he doesn't matter or that he is helpless. It is up to us to give him confidence and independence, and most of all a chance at happiness. Our attitudes about treating everyone with equality can make all the difference."

Unconsciously, he rubbed his thumb over the photograph, saying, "He's perfect to me. Even without speaking or walking, he has so many gestures and expressions. He learns something new every day."

Then there was a silence. I was unsettled by this information. I looked out of the window, thinking how protected and fortunate I was. I could not imagine anything this painful, this permanent. In my short life tragedy had never been part of my experience. I had never known a real crisis. I had been cushioned by loving parents, by financial security, by an abundance of friends and romances. I did everything I wanted to do. There were no obstacles, no hitches. My experience of fear and struggle were limited. I was deeply touched by my companion's capacity for understanding, but more important, I was awed by his graceful acceptance.

I looked into his eyes, then looked again at the photograph of his young son.

"How do the people of your village treat your child?" I asked.

"The people are afraid of handicaps, so they avoid him," he answered. "I don't know why exactly." He stopped, then after a thoughtful pause added, "Maybe they think he has a contagious disease, and if they come too close, they may catch it. It's a kind of superstitious thinking." He hesitated, then sadly murmured, "They're wrong, you know. They're very wrong."

After that I did not know what to say, so I let the silence take over again.

Then as the wheels of the plane touched down on the airstrip at Ithaca airport I suddenly remembered where I was and where I was going. Now it was time for me to enter a world of exciting new possibilities. I hoped I would shake off the unsettled feelings I had from the conversation with the doctor the moment I saw John. I had just enough time to fix my lipstick and comb my hair before disembarking. As we got up from our seats and were standing in the aisle, my companion and I shook hands. Realizing that we would probably not meet again, as we said good-bye I smiled.

"I really enjoyed our talk," I told him, "and I hope for the best for you and your son."

Then he replied, "I wish you happiness and good fortune in your marriage."

When we approached the gate, I spotted John. We both waved frantically above the crowd and laughed as we ran toward each other. We embraced. With my arms wrapped around John, I could see the man from India moving on through the gate. He turned for a moment, glanced back at me and raised his hand in a final farewell.

John's old red Mustang convertible was in the airport parking lot. As we drove to our small furnished basement apartment, I chattered about my parents, about visiting New York City and about all the new items I had purchased for our new home. The apartment was not far from Cornell University where John would be working as a veterinary assistant and I would be taking summer graduate courses toward my masters degree in teaching speech and English.

John was quiet as he listened to my stories. Smiling, he said, "The reason we get along so well is I'm always the listener and you're always the talker."

By the time we arrived at the apartment it was dark. As we dragged the luggage out of the car, John joked about my caravan of suitcases and boxes while I laughed excitedly, defending my need for every item. Struggling into the living room with the luggage, he turned on a lamp. John's clutter was a familiar mess. The apartment was in disarray, but seemed charming despite the fact that clothes were draped over the backs of chairs, magazines and papers were spread everywhere, and the ashtrays were full. I thought to myself, "So what if the cleaning up waits until tomorrow." It just felt good being in our own home that night knowing that we had not only the whole summer but our whole lives ahead of us.

Just then, John surprised me by handing me a bouquet of daisies, my favorite flower. I was touched by the sweetness of his gesture. We continued the celebration by opening a bottle of white wine and, toasting each other, vowed never to leave each other again. Sipping wine, we looked at the bedroom door at the same time. John then carried me gently in his arms and placed me on the bed saying, "I'll love you forever."

"Me too," I said smiling back at him.

Then we both closed our eyes and made love until morning.

I awoke the next morning to find John already dressed and running out the door to work.

"Oh, don't cook tonight," he said. "We're going to celebrate our first twenty-four hours together. I'll take you out for dinner and dancing, like we did on our first date." Then he kissed me and was gone.

The house was strangely quiet when he left. I sat down at the kitchen table to have coffee and my first cigarette of the day. Although I kept promising myself I was going to quit, I loved the routine of starting the morning with coffee and a cigarette. I sat with the stillness of the sun around me and felt the warmth of our home at last. College life had always been so crowded, so rushed, with days of classes at Ithaca College and nights of socializing at Cornell. Now all that was behind me.

I thought of what I would have been doing if I had stayed in Altoona, Pennsylvania with my parents. During the summers past, I had always had a job at my father's distribution company or at his bookstores. But now, having my own life with John seemed so much better. We were a team and we were going to make it by ourselves.

The place was such a mess, I decided to begin by cleaning the bedroom. I rehung all of John's pants and shirts, and sorting through my own clothes, slipped skirts on hangers and dry-ironed my dresses and gowns with the palm of my hand. The closet was soon in meticulous order. Then I made the bed. Without stopping for a breather, I headed for the hallway closet to get the vacuum. As I stooped down to look inside the closet, I suddenly felt dizzy, very dizzy. I fell onto my knees and covered my head with my hands, hoping the dizziness would subside. It was probably due to not getting enough sleep the night before, plus the fact that I had had nothing to eat or drink since lunch, except for the previous night's wine and that morning's coffee. To do all that cleaning on an empty stomach was a miracle in itself. And the morning was hot.

I hauled out the vacuum and a handful of rags that were on the floor of the closet. By 2.30 that afternoon, I had vacuumed the apartment, polished the furniture, cleaned the mirrors and windows and washed the dishes in the sink. When I stopped working the apartment suddenly seemed eerie and very still. I put down the sponge and went into the bedroom. Absentmindedly, I tried to run a brush through my hair. The bristles crackled, upsetting the silence, snapping me into a quick uneasiness. I dropped the brush and toyed with my engagement ring, a little frightened by this new kind of solitude. I looked so tanned and healthy in the mirror, I reached out to touch my own reflection. It gave me a reassuring feeling but the absence of another person made the quiet disturbing. There should have been another person somewhere near, perhaps in another room. I had always lived with someone else, even though I was very independent.

But now I was by myself. Piling my hair on the top of my head and fastening it with a clip, I thought about John. His strong, handsome face was in my mind as I walked into the living room. His books and papers were scattered everywhere. I piled his stacks of papers neatly on the desk and rearranged the daisies in the base. The room began to sparkle as a sense of order was soon restored. I removed a light blue tablecloth, matching napkins and light summer bedroom drapes from one of my suitcases. Disharmony triggered my need to organize and establish efficiency. My eye was very precise, so every painting on the wall had to be adjusted perfectly and all the books had to be arranged by author.

Stooping down to the bottom shelf of the bookcase, I cleared a spot for my journals and papers. I must have stood up too quickly, because a second wave of dizziness swept over me. Gripping the bookcase to steady myself, I rubbed my eyes and pressed my temples, waiting for the feeling to pass. Weakened by this new bout of dizziness, I had to take a break. I sat on the couch with my eyes closed. As the dizziness passed, I slowly opened my eyes and spotted my college diploma on a stack of papers. I was proud to have graduated *Summa Cum Laude*, at the top of my class.

Graduation day was indeed an occasion to remember. It was one of the hottest days of the year and all of the graduating students were sweating and sweltering underneath our black robes. I scanned the vast audience in that immense gym; it looked like an overcrowded basketball game. Rows upon rows of bleachers contained foreign parents from the outside world, all trying to outdo the others with their flashy clothes, smiling their widest grins.

Then the commencement ceremony began. When the first speaker stepped up to the podium, I yawned. By the time we pushed our tassels over from left to right almost three hours had passed. With sighs of relief, we stormed out of the gymnasium like a herd of wild buffalo. All that had happened only three weeks ago, and now I was in Ithaca, preparing for my future life.

Uncertain of my body's reaction to the dizzy spell, I gradually got up and walked over to place my diploma on the mantle. Steadying myself by holding on to the mantle, I felt my strength and balance return and felt good enough to continue cleaning the apartment.

I filed away my teaching resumés and letters of recommendation but first I took one more look at my personal papers. My favorite endorsement of my work was a letter of recommendation from my student teacher supervisor:

Although most student teachers demonstrate bits and pieces of insight, enthusiasm creativity and skill, it is seldom that a student teacher is able to "get it all together" in a brief seven weeks. Barbara is such a student teacher. She is vital and dynamic in her

*teaching, which makes students watch carefully lest they miss some-
thing. Barbara takes a personal interest in her students and manages
to reach some of the "unreachables" by this personal attention.*

I held the letter as if it were alive. Some other statistics listed on
my resumé read: 21-year-old single female. Major: Speech, Drama
and English, with a special emphasis on public speaking. Grade
Point Average: 3.8. Honors: Dean's List. Primary Interests: school
plays, ski team, swimming team, tennis team, cheerleading. Experience: school interviewer, student teacher, teacher's assistant,
actress, suicide prevention counselor and committee chairperson.

Using a map of upstate New York methodically to choose areas
where I could find a teaching job, I applied to over 100 schools and
received 45 positive responses. It was quite a choice, but I selected
a junior high school that would allow me the opportunity to teach
English and to open up my own speech department.

"Enough daydreaming!" I said to myself. It was just after 3.00
and I had to get ready for John, who was due back at 4.00.

In the shower, I let the hot water rush over my body, lathering
my skin. As the soap disappeared in streams off my stomach, I
leaned over to let the water spray down my back. I shampooed and
conditioned my scalp with a milk and honey hair concoction.
After drying myself vigorously, I rubbed cream all over my body.
The hair dryer worked quickly on my hair, and the natural curls
fell softly around my face and down my back. I wondered what I
should wear. Should it be something glamorous, maybe a long silk
gown? I finally opted for a comfortable yet sensual look; a turquoise
halter-neck blouse and a pair of white cut-off shorts. I was about to
put on sandals but decided to go barefoot instead. Now I was ready
for the make-up. Smudging the pencil below my eyes gave me a
sultry look. Next mascara, then a coral cream lipstick that looked
luscious. I fluffed my hair, stood up and walked to the full-length
mirror. The reflection showed me everything was exactly right.

I suddenly realized the time—only 20 minutes before John would
be home. I smiled at the thought of him walking into a transformed
house. Just in time, I remembered to take my birth-control pill; I
usually took it in the morning, but I had forgotten to take it that

day for I had been too busy in my happy trance. I made one more inspection of the apartment. It looked great. Now I was ready for a break and wanted to be in the fresh air. I walked to the corner of the street and spotted a small grocery store. Entering, I decided to buy a bag of cherries. "John and I will take a walk before dinner and eat these," I thought.

John arrived at our apartment a few minutes after I did. He looked around and smiled. "What a transformation! I think I'll keep you. Where do you want to have dinner?"

We decided on a neighborhood restaurant that was known for its pizza and sangria. Seeing that we had plenty of time, we decided to take a walk. I put on my sandals and we headed up the hill towards Cornell.

There was a special feeling walking through our neighborhood for the first time. The street was lined with stone walls that over-looked old quarries filled with water. The quarries were set into a cliff with waterfalls connecting them. The day was cooling off and all we could hear was the sound of water and the wind rustling through the trees. Halfway up the hill, we sat down on a stone wall and watched the golden sun setting over the water.

"Do you want a cherry?" I teased John, dangling one above his lips. He then fed me one, in turn. I was feeling so high that I spit the pit at him and laughed.

"You always keep me surprised," he said. "That's what I love about you."

We stared into the water, lost in our own worlds and comforted by the fact that we shared the same dream. Then we wandered back down to our house to get ready for dinner.

John went into the bathroom when we got back to the apartment and I went to the foot of the bed to step out of my sandals. As I bent down to pull off the left one, it happened. It happened so fast: suddenly I was spiraling down, head first, to the bottom of a well, spinning in perpetual, uncontrolled motion. This dizziness was far worse than the spells that had occurred that morning. It was deep inside my head, as though my brain had gone on a roller-coaster and hadn't bothered to tell the rest of my body. The odd thing is, I never lost consciousness, and I wasn't frightened. It didn't hurt.

There was no pain—no sense of trickling or bursting—just an overwhelming swirling, sharp drop.

As my mind disengaged from my body, it separated the connection between thought and action. Everything now happened in slow motion. My body crumpled. My head hit the wooden floor with a loud thump, and I collapsed on top of it. I could feel the cold, hard planks of the floor. Then there was complete silence. I tried to get up but nothing moved. Something was very wrong. A heaviness, like a man's hand, weighed down on my consciousness, leaving nothing but my will. My will alone tried to pull its companion body back to its rightful place. It tugged at the limp mass and gave a noiseless command to get up. It tried. It strained to push the inert mass on the floor. But there was no mind to assist, no muscle to aid, no words to instruct. Communications were severed. My mind and body could no longer perform its commands. The connection ceased to exist. I didn't know until much later that I had lost the ability to speak.

There was a voice, familiar yet dim. It was John, yelling as he heard the crash.

"Oh my God! What's the matter?" he said, running out of the bathroom. "Oh, my God!"

He bent over me and seeing that I was dazed, gently picked me up and laid me across our bed. He thought I had fainted, so he ran into the kitchen and came back with a paper towel filled with ice. The water trickled down my forehead to my cheeks. It was clear almost at once that ice couldn't fix what was wrong with me. When I didn't respond, John frantically scooped me in his arms and hugging me to his chest, ran to the car.

I wasn't sure why I was placed on the front seat, but when I tried to sit up and look out the window, John pleaded for me to lie down. I couldn't get up anyway, so I lay there, my body moving with the swaying of the car. I didn't wonder or worry abut anything at all. In fact, I didn't even wonder why I couldn't get up. The "I" part of me was lost, the part that reasons, observes and analyzes. My mind had been emptied of words, although I could still watch and feel. I forgot that I knew words, so I did not miss them. Everything was all right. We were going for a ride.

Then the car stopped. The door opened and John left. Now I was alone, confused and uneasy. Then my door opened and John lifted and carried me across gravel that crunched under his feet. The night air was crisp around me. Then we entered a bright, airless room with loud sounds.

"Where's the emergency room?" John shouted to a woman at the desk. Through the noise, a man lifted me out of John's arms, strapped me into a wheelchair, and propelled me down a long white hallway. We went through a doorway into a small cement room. I had no time to think, nor to contemplate whether or not I could think. I just saw everyone hurrying, looking very busy and taking care of me. In contrast, I felt like a child, irresponsible and enjoying it.

I was feeling euphoric, too, for I lost all memory for words referring to the past and future. I was locked in the present, and when you are locked into the present you have no anxieties or cares. My world was the immediate—*now*. And *now* seemed very amusing and attention-getting, with lots of things to watch as they happened. A worried John looked at me, and then asked, "Are you OK Barb?"

I smiled at him innocently.

A man in a long white coat entered the room.

"I'm not going to hurt you," he said softly. "I'm just going to test your reflexes."

He and John propped me up every time I started to slump like a rag doll to one side. I observed my bare feet dangling off the edge of the table as the man in the white coat hit my knees with a small rubber mallet. The right leg twitched a little bit. The left leg jerked a lot. Then he tapped my elbows. Next, he flashed a bright beam in my ears, eyes and mouth. I watched him curiously and giggled. I was not frightened at all, though everyone else seemed to be. But they had the ability to think and were concerned about what happened to me. I no longer had that capability.

"Exactly what happened?" the doctor asked John, as he listened to my heart.

"I don't know," John said. "We went for a walk and we came back to get ready for dinner. She fell. Then she couldn't speak."

"I think your friend has had a stroke. She needs to see a neurologist immediately. We don't have one here at Thompkins County, so I'm going to send her by ambulance to another hospital in Elmira—Arnot-Ogden." The doctor then asked John, "Will you ride with her in the ambulance?"

Before John could reply there were more footsteps. Two people lifted me from the table and onto a narrow bed, strapped two belts tightly across my body and tucked a white blanket around me. Then my bed and I were rolling, and I stared up at an endless line of bright fluorescent lights. Suddenly I was outside again in the cool night air. Someone unbuckled the straps and lifted me onto another bed. This one was softer and had a pillow. Two men slid me into the back of a van and John climbed in beside me. The doors slammed and we began to move. Just at that moment I had to close my eyes. I felt dizzy, as if I was floating. In the distance I heard a voice. Was that John yelling, "Why can't you go any faster?" His tenseness seemed strange. He told me later that it took 45 minutes to reach Elmira; I felt it only took five minutes, as time had no meaning for me.

The next thing I remember is coming to a stop, the van doors opening, and me being lifted onto a hard metal table on wheels. It had no padding and felt cold against my skin. My body was strapped to that coldness. The faces around me looked strange; they were not smiling. Then they disappeared, one by one, as I was rolled under a monstrous metal machine. Someone strapped my head into a contraption, and then I was left there all alone and a long cylinder slid down over me. I couldn't escape. I couldn't even move. I didn't know if anyone was there. I had to lie still while this machine came at me, rotating and scanning my entire face, body and brain. That's when I realized something must be seriously wrong. I felt my first moment of panic and fear.

Breathing was difficult inside this machine. Did the people who put me there not know this? The cylinder began to move to one side and stopped. It clicked. Then with a soft whir it rotated and stopped. It clicked again. Whir, stop, click . . . whir, stop, click. Then there appeared a pane of tinted glass and a thin green line of light. I watched the light move, and was hypnotized by it so much that I began to feel like part of the machine. Then it suddenly pulled back toward the ceiling, leaving me exposed. Someone came to take me out of the harness I had been trapped in. And without warning I was pushed out of the room into a sea of light, noise and faces.

I felt exhausted by the bombardment of competing sensations. It seemed as if the filter that screened what poured into my brain had been destroyed. My senses overwhelmed me with panic. I couldn't take the bright light or noise. Yet as suddenly as it had started, the clamor went away. The people in white wheeled me into a large, quiet gray room. There I was transferred onto a hard bed. Chrome bars were pulled up around me and the curtain was half drawn, separating me from the others. In the far distance, I saw a middle-aged women in a white cap sitting at a desk. Then someone pricked me with a needle. That was the last think I remembered as I drifted off.

During the next few days in the intensive care ward, the frightening, lonely feelings came back to haunt me as nightmares. But the worst nightmare was waking up to find that I did not feel or look or act like myself any more. I had gone from healthy to handicapped in an instant, from "one of us" to "one of them," from being a full member of the human race to being an outsider, a reject. That was the source of my deepest terror.

Was the flight to Ithaca the night before an omen? With the doctor I met on the plane, I had discussed the prejudices and tragedy that affect the disabled. Suddenly I had joined their ranks and would have to live on the other side of humanity for the rest of my life. How ironic that at the young age of 21 I should suffer a stroke. I was so vital and healthy, and had never even been in a hospital. Now I would have to live out my life with this painful and deforming tragedy, just like the doctor's young son. And society would choose whatever negative labels it saw fit to apply to me, for the rest of my life. I would be forced to become an outcast. People would say, "She is disabled" and ignore my mind, my feelings and my soul. I would be banished from society, and not a trace of the old me would ever be found.

CHAPTER ONE

Disconnected

While I slept, John was waiting outside the ward for my mother. He had called her from the hospital, saying, "Barbara fell and she couldn't get up!"

"What do you mean, she fell?", my mother asked, terrified.

"All I know is that she fell and then she couldn't talk. We had just returned from a walk and were getting ready to go out to dinner when it happened."

Confused and alarmed my mother said, "What do you mean she can't talk?"

"I don't know anything more," John answered. "A neurologist is looking at her now."

"She needs a neurologist!" my mother said. "I'll be there as soon as I can. Please, John, stay with her. Do not for any reason leave her for a moment. Please stay with her. Do you hear me?"

My mother had been alone when the call came; my father was away on business. Earlier, he had spoken to her from Pittsburgh airport. Because it was so late and he was tired, they decided that he should stay the night in a hotel near the airport and come home in the morning. They hung up before my mother had a chance to ask which hotel he was planning on staying in. She thought about how they had supported and helped each other through every crisis during their 25-year marriage. Now she had only herself to rely on, and it was imperative to act quickly.

She started dialing hotels in an attempt to locate my father but became frustrated after a dozen attempts. As it was getting later and later, she knew she would have to leave the house and go to the hospital alone. The next call she made was to her neighbor, Gail. After telling her what she knew, my mother asked Gail if she would be willing to drive her to Elmira, and Gail agreed. Immediately after she'd hung up, the phone rang. My mother's heart jumped, believing it was a call from my father. However, it was Dr Greenwald, the neurologist in Elmira.

"I have just been with your daughter and examined her. She's awake and alert, but uncoordinated and unable to speak."

Shaken, my mother asked, "What's wrong with my daughter?"

"Mrs. Newborn," Dr. Greenwald explained, "your daughter has suffered a stroke. It's rare in people her age. It is the type of stroke that happens to older people."

"Is she in pain, doctor?"

"No, she's not. As a matter of fact, she is quite comfortable. She is in the intensive care unit where we're watching her very carefully. There is a paralysis of her right leg and arm, but we don't know if that is permanent or temporary."

After hanging up, my mother began to write a note to my father. She repeated what the doctor had just reported and included the address and telephone number of the hospital. She ended the note by saying he should meet her there as soon as possible. Alone with her thoughts, she kept thinking, "What has happened to my Barbara, her wonderful plans, and her love of life?" It was impossible for her to believe that her beautiful daughter couldn't even speak and that she was lying in a hospital bed paralyzed.

Early the next morning, I awoke, as if in a dream, to find my mother standing over the bed. I knew her as if by instinct, sensing her instantly. She sat on the edge of the bed and took me in her arms. Cradling me, with her soothing voice, she said over and over again, "Oh, my darling, you're going to be all right. You're going to get better!"

She was the first person to hold me, to warm me, in that whole time of being poked and prodded and wheeled around on stretchers and rolled under those cold, hard machines. Something broke in me. Something reminded me that I was attached to someone, someone who cared. I was reminded that I hadn't always been a disconnected body lost in a bed. And, like a baby protected by her mother's loving care, I was cradled and lulled to sleep once more.

A few hours later, the people in white woke me up. Being awakened by these strangers confused me. Then someone pulled the privacy curtain around the bed. Surrounding me were beds in a row, separated and sectioned off by other drawn curtains. I was afraid because some of the people in those cots looked scary, like mummies, bandaged from head to toe. All I knew was that I didn't belong here and I had to get out. In my tormented mind, I again wondered what I was doing here. Not one of the people in white told me why I was here! Their tones and looks only worsened my bewilderment, for there was pity in their voices.

My father soon entered the room with my mother at his side. In the past I had always relied on my father's strength and confidence, but now his face reflected worry and uncertainty. From his expression, I sensed that I could no longer look to him for answers. I was entering this new world alone.

In the intensive care unit, I had no reminders or connections to who I once was. The institutional machines and colorless walls created a sterile, cold atmosphere, void of familiar associations. Instead of recalling my love of life with warmth and color, it desensitized me. From now on, the people in white dominated this unfamiliar environment. They were responsible for my every need, controlling my every movement from toilet functions to bathing to feeding. Just like a Raggedy Anne doll, I was numb, muddled and totally passive, unaware that I was capable of movement by myself. The people in white did it all for me. They were both my rescuers and my imprisoners.

I had no memory of how I had once functioned. With my mind in a daze and the paralysis leaving me with no feeling on my right side, there was nothing to remind me that I was once right-handed. After all, the only thing I was required to do was lie in bed; no one encouraged me to move. I was even unaware that movement in my right leg and foot had begun to return until the next day, when my neurologist, Dr Greenwald, came to check if I had made any progress. He asked me to try moving my leg up and down and to wiggle my toes. When I did this, he smiled and said how impressed he was that I was doing so well. He was the first person to speak and smile at me with confidence and optimism. He genuinely seemed to care.

Still smiling, he turned to my parents and said that it was his professional opinion that I should now be moved to a private room. I no longer had to be watched on a 24-hour basis. He then added that by the end of the week, I could continue my recovery at home. There I would receive the love and support I needed. With that, he winked at me and said, "In no time at all you're going to be just fine." And then he left.

On the fifth day of my hospital stay, I was moved from the intensive care unit to a sunny room with open drapes, a mirrored dresser, a color TV and a bed without any bars at the sides. After the sterile atmosphere of the unit this new room reflected amiable, well-known feelings of my past life. My family and fiancé were waiting there and greeted me with love and presents. Now, bathed in embraces, I was able to smile for the first time in days.

One of the gifts was a drawing pad with crayons. Everyone was standing around me as I positioned the pad in my lap and fumbled to open the box of crayons. Excitedly, I was ready to draw a really happy picture of myself in a pretty dress, barefoot, as I ran through wild flowers and green fields. But I hesitated. In the past I had always been able to draw my thoughts. Why couldn't I do that now? What was wrong with me? Was it not being used to using my left hand, or was it something more?

It seemed as if my subconscious was struggling with my conscious. They were in conflict for some unknown reason. My left hand picked up a red crayon and, as if it had a will of its own started printing the misspelled, though legible words,

I can't believe it happened to me.

I looked, disbelieving, at what I had written. My subconscious had finally won by writing the reality I couldn't face. Surrounded by my family in this safe, protected place, I could finally release all the feelings that had been buried in me for five days. I began remembering the pain and laughter of who and what I had been.

I spent two more days in that private room. As long as I was with people who loved me, especially John, everything seemed as it should be. On the eighth and final day of my stay, John and I took a stroll. He pushed me in the wheelchair and we rolled down the long hospital corridors, laughing and clowning. I just accepted that from now on it would always be like this, with John and me happy together. But just then, my father approached us, and said, "Well, it's time to say good-bye, for now."

I looked at John, wondering what my father meant. My father looked serious, and the laughter was gone. Then he leaned down, facing me, and said softly, "Look, Sugar, we're going home and John can't come with us."

I still didn't understand. I was dazed when John kissed me and said, "Look, I'll see you in Pennsylvania in less than ten days. Don't worry, I'll be there."

The tears started to roll down my cheeks as I began to comprehend that I was no longer my parents' willful, independent daughter. I realized I could no longer control my own world. Scared, I had trouble breathing. I needed air.

I was being forced to let go of John and our dream, and there was nothing I could do. He had been with me through all of this and now he would be gone, as though he had never be a part of me at all. He had been with me to put me on the bed. He had been with me to drive me to the hospital. He had been with me during that ambulance ride. And now I felt the pain and loneliness of having to leave him behind.

When my father's car pulled up around the circular driveway, I was wheeled through the hospital doors and into the car by an attendant, who lifted and secured me gently into the back seat. The door was then shut and locked. With my father at the wheel and my mother again at his side, the car started and we were off—to where I did not know. Turning to see John slowly disappear into the blurred distance was the hardest good-bye I had ever experienced. It was a powerless good-bye, filled with the fear that came from not knowing what was to become of me. I didn't even know where we were going. And I couldn't stop crying.

CHAPTER TWO

Prison

In my past, crying was unfamiliar to me. I tried wiping the tears streaming down my face with my right hand, but in spite of my efforts my hand refused to move. My head was propped up against a large, soft pillow and my body was covered with a thin, white blanket. Embarrassed, I now had no choice but to let my tears soak into the pillow, hoping my parents wouldn't see.

All the medication I was given kept me half-dozing in the back seat, waking sporadically to feel the sun's gentle heat through the window. In what seemed to be a short while, the car stopped in front of a house. The ride was seven hours long but I didn't notice.

I wanted to feel secure in the knowledge that my parents were never going to let anything happen to me again. My father, smiling, turned to me and said, "Well, darling, we're finally home."

Looking out the window, I was confounded. I did not belong here. Why were they taking me here anyway? Then my parents left the front seat to help me out; first one leg, then the other, in slow motion. I had trouble standing up in this new body and being cramped in one position for so long had made me stiff.

Several strangers were coming out of houses, approaching us. It was frightening, since I didn't recognize any of them. My father took a crutch out of the car and gently handed it to me. Leaning on the side of his Oldsmobile, I placed it under my left arm. I felt these strangers starting to crowd us as I slowly followed my parents toward the back door. Some of them helped me walk. Other people gave me get-well cards and flowers. This outpouring of attention was overwhelming and made me understand how extensively my mind had been impaired. Not only was I locked into the present, but I had also lost the capacity to sift and put my thoughts and feelings into order. Bombarded by everything being thrown at me all at once I just wanted to be left alone.

As soon as I entered the silence of my parents' home, the chaos stopped. The house seemed cold and strange. Instinctively I let go of the crutch and I put my good arm around myself for protection and slowly made my way up the stairs. Obviously my body no longer responded the way it once did. My right leg was heavy and numb, as if it had been replaced by weights much too heavy for me to lift. When I finally reached the top step, I was exhausted. I sensed that I had been here before and yet it felt like a new experience.

"Could this be my old room?" I thought. The familiarity brought me comfort, but the room seemed unusually distant, as if I were looking at it through a reversed telescope.

I entered to find a full-length mirror in front of me. I was startled to see myself for the first time. My eyes couldn't blink, nor did they sparkle the way they used to. I stared, as a small child would, at the lifeless figure before me. Although I had completely forgotten what I looked like, I knew that this face and body didn't seem like me at all. I must have stared at her for at least 20 minutes but still the figure in front of me didn't change. Her face was distorted and disfigured. She had a wordless mouth, a dark hole stuck in her face. The mouth couldn't smile or show its teeth. It couldn't frown, yawn, or even stick out its tongue.

I began to undress, using only my left hand. Pulling up my polo shirt I saw my breasts. They were foreign, red and ugly.

"They couldn't be *my* breasts," I thought. They had to belong to someone else. I didn't recognize them. All the same, I couldn't help staring at their strangeness.

My hair was all matted and knotty and it smelled, so I picked up a brush from the dresser and began brushing my hair. As I did so, I noticed the stranger in the mirror also brushing *her* hair! The synchronized action was mesmerizing and as I watched in fear, we brushed our hair together. Then I began crying, softly, helplessly. I didn't want to deal with this stranger yet. Not now . . . not ever! I hated her! I wasn't like her at all.

"I was pretty," I told myself. "This deformity isn't me! Why won't she leave me alone?"

Then I heard my mother's voice in the distance saying, "Sweetheart, do you need anything?"

As she entered the room I grabbed a nightgown from the dresser to cover myself. However, I found myself losing control as I let her put it on me. It was as if she were dressing a baby, and I was immediately thrown back into a loving but very dependent, child–parent relationship. Before all this had happened I had been so independent. Yet the adult feelings of love that John and I had once shared were nowhere to be found. I was now entirely dependent on others in so many ways. I allowed my mother to tuck me into bed without putting up a fight, which was odd. She then turned off the light and, propping a pillow under my limp arm, kissed me goodnight. I was very tired and soon fell fast asleep, but I did not dream.

The following morning I was greeted by my mother's cheerful voice. "Wake up dear. You have an hour until we have to be at the Altoona hospital. Your father just came out of the shower so you can use it now. It's all yours."

Her light-hearted voice was a sharp contrast to my feelings. I was groggy but it was not from a bad night's sleep. I felt drugged, different. Nothing was familiar inside or outside of me. I had no center, no balance, no personal reference to anything meaningful.

I stumbled out of bed and made my way across the hallway and into the bathroom. Switching on the light with my left hand was difficult since this hand was not used to much activity, except to help my right hand when it needed assistance. Now I would have to explore my own way of doing simple tasks, like taking a shower. Out of desperation and necessity I was forced to reinvent how I would do things that had taken me no time at all before the stroke. I would have to use all my strength and ingenuity just to put on a shower cap. Grabbing the elastic cap off the towel ring, I tried putting it on with my one and only useful hand. As I lowered my head into it, my hair came tumbling down around me. My independent nature fiercely informed me that I would have to try doing this another way. Biting down hard on the front end of the shower cap while holding the back end with my left hand, I proceeded to fit my head into the cap. It worked. But instead of feeling triumph, I felt an overwhelming sadness for my defeated right hand. I defiantly removed the cap and slowly turned on one faucet at a time, stepped into the shower and let the water spray on me. Clutching the bar of soap in fear of dropping it, I barely managed to wash the front of my body. And now only one hand could reach when it came to washing the back.

I could not remember the last time I had washed my hair, so I attempted to shampoo it. Picking up the bottle, I unscrewed the top with my teeth but the bottle fell, spilling the contents. I had to get out of there because I wanted to slide down to the shower floor and cry. Turning off the water, I stepped out and tried to put a towel around me but it slipped off my body. Dripping wet and cold, I pulled a robe off the bathroom door but was unable to get the buttons through the proper holes and the robe hung open. Then I saw the bathroom scale and stepped on it. I could neither read the numbers nor remember what I had weighed before.

Quickly, I looked around for something familiar and spotted a can of spray deodorant. But I soon discovered that it was impossible for me to use it because it meant holding it and pushing with my finger. Next, I tried to use the toothbrush. Again, here was another new task. I had to unscrew the toothpaste cap by biting down hard and turning the tube with my left hand. My teeth would now have to do what my right hand had once done.

While brushing, I had a strange sensation. The right side of my mouth was numb. Aggravated, I slammed down the toothbrush and picked up the mouthwash. Pouring the liquid into my mouth made me choke. I immediately spat it out. The muscles in my mouth and throat were paralyzed. It then struck me—these were my speech muscles!

Staring into the mirror I knew I could no longer do any of the things that as a young woman I had always taken for granted, like setting my hair or polishing and filing my nails. I couldn't wear eye make-up any more unless I learned to apply it with my left hand. But even so, how was I going to open the eye shadow container? I needed two hands. And how was I going to use the eyeliner? I couldn't even draw a straight line on my lid. And anyway, I had no idea how to hold the eyeliner brush. Mascara was impossible to apply with my left hand alone and it felt strange putting the rouge on the numb side of my face. Everything I did was mixed up and seemed wrong.

Feeling dizzy and weak, I went back to my bedroom and collapsed on the bed. The room began to spin as soon as I closed my eyes. I was exhausted and frustrated, but tried to build up enough strength to get dressed. I knew getting dressed would be even more draining. No longer knowing where anything was, I forced myself to the bureau. My head began to hurt but I did not give in to the way I felt. Opening a drawer, I found some undergarments. With my good arm I managed to put on a bra, but couldn't hook it. I had to find another way. With the support of my right elbow lying flat against my right side to hold the elastic band in place, my left hand was able to pull the left side of the band over until it met with the right. After many attempts I hooked it in place.

Now I had to tackle the underpants. I must have looked like a girdle ad, putting them on with only one hand. The elastic waistband was as difficult to pull up as a girdle, and I had a struggle getting into it. Next, I had to pick out a skirt from a closet full of clothes. I drew a blank; I did not know which one to choose. Yanking one out, I realized I couldn't zip it with only one hand so, despairing, I dropped it. Rummaging through a drawer, I managed to find elastic-banded shorts and a tee-shirt. With much difficulty, I was at last able to get them on. Then, when I finally thought I was ready go downstairs, I looked down and noticed my bare feet. Heartbroken, I realized that I couldn't wear my sneakers, since they had laces. Now it was necessary to find a pair of slip-on shoes. As I turned off the bedroom light I caught one last look at the mess I would have to clean up when I came home from the hospital. My mother would have been prepared to clean up for me but I insisted that I would do it myself.

In the past, I used to run down the stairs; now I had to take one step at a time. It must have taken all of fifteen minutes just to get to the bottom step, where it was necessary to rest. Finally I made it to the breakfast table in the next room.

Watching my mother set the table for breakfast baffled me because I had no idea what all those utensils lined up on both sides of the plate were for. I sat down as she went to get things from the refrigerator and came back with half a cold cantaloupe. I looked at her and then the plate. She watched me and then placed a spoon in my left hand. There was silence for a moment. Ready, utensil in hand, I dug in, but I was at a loss how to get the fruit out. I butchered it, since I was unable to ask for help. While I struggled to force the spoon out, the melon slid to the floor. I looked down at the smashed melon like a toddler. My mother walked over, smiling, and cleaned up the mess. In a reassuring tone she said to me, "I'll cut it into bite-size pieces for you from now on. But you have to eat something now. How about some cheese with bread and butter?"

I voicelessly watched her butter the bread and bring it to the table with some orange juice, served with a straw. I was at a loss; all I could do was lean my head over the table and sip through the straw. I couldn't even trust the strength in my left hand to pick up the glass. After all this, I didn't feel like eating any more.

Feeling despondent, my vision blurred and teary, I wondered, "Will it always be this way with me?"

If so, I couldn't live like this. I was scared being inside this body, inside this prison. I was no longer me. My body was no longer my body; my mind was no longer my mind. I felt like Humpty Dumpty—we had both had a bad fall. Would they ever be able to put me back together again? I was going to find out when I began my therapy.

CHAPTER THREE

A Puppet with Broken Strings

Journal entry:

This terribly frightened little girl is walking on a tightrope. But you're going to be yourself, provided you walk the full length. It's a very long rope with various turns, making it more difficult, but you must be strong enough to face the challenges. Each day you come one step further to your destination. You may at times not see the progress—but it is really there. And that glorious day when you need not walk any farther, you will look back and see that this hellish nightmare you are having now never existed at all.

On my first day of outpatient therapy at Altoona's Mercy Hospital, 17 June, my mother drove me there but I insisted on entering the building alone. I had to maintain some dignity. Hesitantly, using a cane, I made my way to the check-in room, which was really a wall with a circular hole cut in it. That opening was meant for private talk and the exchange of papers. But since I couldn't speak, I had to present my blue ID card mutely every day or they would have no record I was ever there. That was all I had to show my attendance and progress. My total importance was embodied in this card, which now signified my new life.

When the receptionist pointed toward where I was to go, I awkwardly made my way down a long disinfectant-smelling corridor until I came to what looked like a big gymnasium. In the middle of the floor lay all sorts of equipment: stationary bicycles, weights, and high cushioned tables. Against the wall were benches, whirlpool baths, curtained shower stalls and straight wooden chairs. Standing there helplessly, I waited for someone to give me instructions since my head was empty of thought. I wasn't there more than a few seconds when out of nowhere came a resounding voice, "Well, so you're Barbara Newborn!"

Walking toward me with great strides was a large, gray-haired woman. Reaching me, she continued in a more subdued tone, "I'm Thelma, head of the physical therapy department. Don't worry, we'll have you back in shape in no time."

Not having any words to say, I smiled politely. Then Thelma instructed two therapists to give me a three-hour series of tests. I was more than happy to let them take over responsibility for my body. They measured my ability to lift leg and arm weights, pedal a bicycle, hop on one foot, stand to attention, walk blindfolded down a room, do jumping-jacks and touch my toes with my hands. It was just like a high-school gym test, except this time I did not do so well. Whether I was lifting leg weights or running on a tread-mill, my clumsy body got in its own way. My coordination and judgment were so poor I couldn't do a simple maneuver. I no longer had spatial awareness, nor could I tell where my body began and ended. It was as though my mind, body and environment were all parts of the same dimension.

I tried to imagine myself performing as I used to but I couldn't see all the necessary steps. All I had were partial memories of the way I used to be but without words—just broken pieces of me which faded in and out of focus. Now it was impossible for me to form an image of my body. I knew that it used to be supple, strong and always freely moving. I was one of those people who couldn't sit still. My friends would always ask me if I had ants in my pants. Laughing, I would stick out my tongue at them and keep on moving. I just loved my body to be in perpetual motion, whether I was doing somersaults in the backyard or playing football with the boys. But now I wouldn't even be picked to keep the score.

It seemed I could not coordinate my arm and leg movements or even walk right. How did they expect me to manage stairs, with weights on my legs no less? As I tried to perform this maneuver, my right arm stubbornly clung to my side. It was as if it wanted to help by giving my leg extra support and strength. But strangely, nothing really disturbed or annoyed me as long as I was with the therapists. In fact, it all rather amused me.

Preparing for the next step, the therapists strapped me into a chair and wheeled me out to the occupational therapy room. At last I was sitting down, but why did they have to bind me? They even insisted on putting a blanket over my legs to seal me up so that I would be ready for delivery to someone else on another floor. Still, I was relatively content to be controlled and carted everywhere. I was then rolled to the elevator and spun around to face it. Leaning forward, my attendant gave me a cheery grin. Unable to say anything witty, I just grinned back like the Cheshire cat. Then, after an awkward wait, the elevator finally arrived. When the thick metallic doors opened I felt myself being jerked backwards and forwards, then backwards again.

A female therapist wheeled me down a hallway to a corner room whose door was ajar. As we neared it, I grew excited, noticing that the room looked inviting. It had big picture windows letting in light, which spread across the nicely polished floors. Spanning the entire length of the wall was a huge mirror with a metal bar attached to its center, like those in ballet classes. There was also a large, round table covered with Chinese checkers, tennis balls, dominoes and beanbags.

Another woman, dressed in white, stood up and warmly greeted me in a funny accent. Oddly enough, her accent put me at ease with my own weird speech. I felt instantly connected and smiled, wondering if we had met before. There was a strong sense of warmth and familiarity about her. Walking toward me, she said confidently, "I'm Teresa, and also your parents' next-door neighbor."

Was she a part of that stampede that greeted me the day of my arrival at my parents' house? I hoped not! But everything was such a blur that day, I could not remember. She continued as I sat dumbfounded. "We will meet here every day for two months, and if you like, we can also get together at your parents' home."

That afternoon I felt a surge of confidence. I wished that somehow Teresa would turn out to be a conjurer or Mother Teresa in disguise and that by some magic of the imagination, I would instantly be returned to the Barbara of the past. But she was just an ordinary person with no magic to offer that day. Her therapy started off with us playing with children's toys, practicing exercises and making childish faces at each other. She had a warm sense of humor and a cheerful optimism that added a bright spot to the challenges of therapy. Because she shared whatever we did, I did not have to be alone in confronting my body. We tried bouncing tennis balls, threading thick-needled yarn, placing marbles in a Chinese checker board, throwing beanbags in imaginary circles and squeezing silly putty in our fists.

After that, things became much more serious and difficult. Now I had to move my right hand without Teresa's help. Placing it flat on the table and separating my fingers, she at first gently and patiently worked each one forward and backward. Then, one at a time, she told me to touch my thumb to the tips of my fingers as if they were made of rubber. When I couldn't do this, she took over. Continuing in a strangely silent, detached way, I observed as she continued working on wrist-turning, elbow-bending and arm-circling. It was as if I was watching a movie of myself.

Next, she secured my hand in a glove which had bright red leather fingers. Attached to each tip was a thick rubber band strung to the palm. Teresa told me the aim of this exercise was to strengthen my fingers by opening my hand. No matter how many times I tried, however, it would not stretch those bands. It just lay there. Then my fingers crawled back into a fist, as if to hide.

Alone I did not have the necessary strength—I wanted Teresa to become a part of me. She continued to be encouraging as we worked with a hard plastic ball with buttons. I tried to press them down with my right fingers but couldn't. Seeing how weak my right hand really was, I compared it with my left, with which I could press the buttons down with ease. The difference was startling, and she quickly placed my arm back in the sling which had become its refuge.

For the last task, Teresa guided me over to a mirror. I tried following her instructions to make faces as I looked at my distorted reflection. At first it was funny watching me trying to imitate everything she did. We were like a comedy team; she was the straight person, with her perky Spanish accent, and I was the funny one, like Harpo Marx.

As best I could, I raised one eyebrow, blinked each eye, smiled so that all my teeth showed, frowned, wrinkled my forehead and wiggled my nose. But I could not really make the funny faces she did. One side was frozen into position and didn't move. It didn't do anything; it just hung there with a blank expression, like a classical theater mask with the other side smiling.

I examined the stranger's face again. I knew I hadn't looked like this before the stroke. I used to be so proud of the way I looked. I walked in the streets with perfect clothes on my attractive figure and, sweeping my head back, I would make my hair bounce. Whenever I passed a man, he'd smile and look again and I'd return a charming smile to him. All of that was gone now. Now no one would ever see that again! As I focused back on the mirror, it was ironic to hear Teresa say, "Now pucker up that mouth, like a kiss."

After completing that first day of therapies I must have looked like a puppet with broken strings; I certainly felt that way. I had been shown what I did not want to know: that my body was a reject, a perfect companion for my mind. Feeling depleted and cast aside, I waited in the hospital entrance for my mother to pick me up and drive me home. There were no distractions and I had only myself for company, but that was not enough. I felt as though a big wind was toppling me over and I did not have the strength or the resources to get up. Instead, people would just walk on, not caring that my body was on the floor. After all, my time was up with the professionals and they had gone on to other patients.

As my mother drove me home, I stared silently in front of me with all those feelings locked inside. Words took too much effort and my speech would have come out as a monotonous noise anyway.

Throughout the summer my outpatient rehabilitation took at least half of each day. Indeed I had the challenge of my life: whether I was going to live or die this way. I received three different types of therapy at the hospital. The rest of my time was spent at home practicing my exercises. The schedule was exhausting and often lasted 14 hours a day. Needing to be totally consumed by therapy, I spent many hours trying to regain my strength, coordination and endurance. I tried to force my body to obey my will and had to push myself constantly to regain what I had lost. Sometimes it took all my determination and faith to keep from giving up.

Every day I would set a different goal: lifting one more pound, moving a different hand muscle, or completing a sentence without stumbling. Driven by a distant memory of the way things used to be, I was convinced that as long as I made progress, I would be myself in no time. But there were so many facets to being disabled and I was only beginning to enter this world where I had so much to learn. I had to discipline myself in a totally new way, learning everything all over again, constantly adapting, adjusting or doing without. Using a pair of scissors, buttering bread, cutting meat, even handling money was a chore. My math was awful. Counting on my fingers, twice if necessary, was the only way I could add and subtract. The image of my broken self was emotionally unbearable. But more devastating was my lost voice. With the terrible isolation of aphasia I did not have any words to echo how I felt.

CHAPTER FOUR

Stranger in a Strange Land

Journal entry:

I'm really worried that I won't get back my language. There are deficiencies in the following:

1 *I have trouble with spelling.*
2 *Poor vocabulary.*
3 *I can get the main message across, but I have trouble finding the exact words.*
4 *My attention span is less.*
5 *I use many opposites—when I want to say "in" I say "out".*
6 *I have trouble describing something in detail whether it's a story or a dream.*
7 *I slur words.*

I've also been told in a book about strokes, unless the aphasic patient recovers in six months, chances are he won't. I have until December 7, the day Pearl Harbor was bombed.

Aphasia was the major destructive force that isolated me from the rest of the world. It destroyed all my connections with others. Being physically disabled was a loss, but losing my language was a disaster. I had been a speech and English major ever since the tenth grade. Now I became obsessed with regaining my ability to communicate. There was always the problem of what to say and how to say it, of deliberately choosing, arranging and speaking the words that best expressed my ideas. At first I was not able to read even at the simplest level or to write a word. It was as though my mind had been emptied of words and their meanings. I could not think in sentences and could barely hold simple images in my mind before they faded away.

I felt absolutely terrorized by the idea of a future without speech and could only try to manage as best as I could in the present. Every day I waited, nervous and excited, for the half-hour speech-therapy lesson. And every tiny bit of progress became a real accomplishment, particularly when I learned to speak one more word. Working my way to the end of a children's story book or trying to relate to my father in words during our morning walks became vital to me. But at times I was overwhelmed and grew angry and cried. I even sometimes slammed doors or threw objects—all because of a terrible, overwhelming sense of frustration and loneliness at being unable to communicate with anyone, including myself at times.

Communicating in verbal language separates us from all other animals. This unique ability gives us shape and defines us. But for the person with aphasia, all that is lost, cut down in a single moment. The aphasic patient makes a sudden transition from the position of a thinking, speaking adult to that of a one-year-old.

As babies, we start listening to the world around us. By the age of two we are beginning to formulate language and are not conscious of the developmental steps. The person with aphasia must struggle with this process. Unlike the infant, whose cognition and language suit each other, the inside of the aphasic mind conflicts with the outward expression of the spoken word. Because the intellect is still intact, the aphasic is easily frustrated and very aware that his communication abilities are damaged.

Language loss alters the aphasic's self-image, affecting relationships with others. He is painfully aware that others don't understand what he's trying to communicate. This makes him especially insecure about his speaking. Voice production and statements are always a matter of special concern, anxiety and effort.

He must always worry about what he is going to say, how to say it, and how to keep command of it.

The aphasic must carefully choose each word and then plan how to form, arrange and utter them. Precise thoughts overload mind and speech is usually so slurred that a stranger might wonder if he is drunk. His language difficulties are overwhelming and complicated. Because of this, speech can no longer be spontaneous. Normal speakers can keep their minds on the concepts to be communicated and form their statements very rapidly. But the slowness and deliberateness of the aphasic underlines the complexity of speech production. A communication malfunction in his brain creates severe problems in controlling language. Only if the aphasic is able to find some way of external expression can he think about socializing and declaring some identity in the world.

An analogy is to imagine yourself a stranger in a foreign land, not knowing the customs or the language. Your vocabulary might be limited to a few words—not even enough to order food or ask for directions. Your first utterance would be a conscious, effort-ridden response. A native, not comprehending what you were trying to say, would be apt to interrupt or even ignore you, and you would feel lost, alien and helpless as a result. Such is the case with aphasics. They are always strangers in a strange land.

Suddenly I was a foreigner, even in my own home. At first I could not even communicate simple requests or my slightest thoughts or needs. I couldn't even laugh. It felt as if my whole personality had been destroyed. Now I was lost and alone within myself. It seemed as if no one would ever know Barbara Newborn again but me. And in time, I would forget because I had no sentences to remind me. I did not have words yet, or connected ideas to express who I was or what I was feeling. My whole personality was gone.

The first few hours after the stroke I didn't miss the sound of my voice. I was completely carefree and without any worries—euphoric, because with no words I had no past or future. My awareness was confined to the immediate present. My world was frozen. I could not remember what had happened yesterday and did not know the meaning of tomorrow. I was lost in some unknown dimension of my own mind. But the last day in the hospital, my language loss devastated me. Suddenly I realized that I couldn't connect with John or my father to express feelings or even the simplest thoughts.

On 21 June, the fourteenth day of my recovery, something exciting happened. The first clear image was in my mind when I awoke from my daytime nap. It was that of an ice cream cone. I didn't know what it was at first, since my mind had lost all its past labels. But the vision would not go away. It kept re-entering my mind. It was here and then it was gone and then it reappeared again as a white, creamy substance, swirled in a light brown funnel. With this image, I felt a painful emptiness in my stomach. What did this image have to do with this emptiness? Yes! Yes, that was it. I was hungry. I desired it. I wanted to eat it right away! But how could I. For I no longer knew how to get what I wanted.

That instant I hopped on my legs and mimicked charades. I jumped up and down waving my arms frantically. I looked at my mother to see if she was watching. She was. So I began my mindless pantomime, with my hollowed mouth ejecting:

"I-i-i. . .

"I-i-i-ie-e. . .

"I-i-i-ie . . . i-i-i-iiiccc. . .

"Iicece. . .

"Iieec. . .

"I-i-i. . .

"I-i-i-ie-e. . ."

I kept on waving her on to read my thoughtless mind. I did not know what else to do. I did not have the proper tools for speech. All I could do was wave my arms expressively. Finally I just stood there, miserable and exhausted with bombarding confusion. My mind had emptied out again. The image of the ice cream cone was lost, all forgotten, there were no more words. Would it return or not? Just then my mother, getting up from her chair, said thoughtfully, "Ice . . . ice cream cone? Do you want an ice cream cone?"

I happily nodded my head up and down and, like a dog, was rewarded for my tricks.

My first word was when I was a child was "baby." I do not

remember any past before that. When that first word came, I would say it over and over again. I liked the sound of my voice getting instant publicity and success, and all the adults would say, "Ah, isn't she cute?" as I mimicked and formed all the sounds I heard. Now, my very first word as a person of 21 gave me just such a warm sense of accomplishment. I knew that one day I would be able to speak again like the person I had been—or would I?

Two days later, I began speech therapy at the hospital. The therapist would be the first person I could talk to—for half an hour each day. The wait in the waiting room seemed endless, although it must have been no longer than 15 minutes. Next to me was a long table scattered with magazines. But, unable to read, I just sat there, staring.

An elderly couple was seated across from me. A husband and wife it seemed, for they both had the same stern, concerned look on their faces and the same gestures. The man had a cane, and when he finally got up, he limped with it. His right arm was stiff and attached to his side. His hand was in a tight fist, just a knotted ball without any dimension to his fingers. When their name was called, they went out of the waiting room. Then my turn came.

I hobbled down a long narrow corridor, passing many closed doors with illegible signs on them. A pretty blonde-haired woman stood in front of one. She smiled and patiently waited for me. "Good morning, Barbara. My name is Kathleen."

Her speech was so exact and precise, I yearned to talk with the same precision when I heard it.

The room was big, with open windows that let in the sun. It had the appearance of a child's room, a kindergarten, with a cheerful atmosphere and all sorts of board games sprawled out on the floor. Also, like Teresa's room, there was a long mirror and a blackboard taking up one whole wall. The furniture consisted of a low, round, pastel yellow table with matching chairs. The chairs were in disorder for they had recently been occupied by children.

Kathleen had me sit down next to her, and together we played a simple game. She asked me a series of questions, and I was to squeeze her hand once for yes and twice for no.

"Are you living in Altoona, Pennsylvania?"

I squeezed her hand once.

"Do you have parents?"

I responded the same way.

"Can you speak?"

I pleadingly squeezed her hand "no."

She then gave me a series of diagnostic tests to measure my aptitude as an "aphasic victim." For the second time, my whole worth was on a piece of paper. These tests consisted in matching words to pictures, matching letters to forms, repeating sentences and digits, and recognizing letters. But I just couldn't recognize those letters, so how was I to recognize sentences? I couldn't identify items or follow directions. And if I could not comprehend the written word, how could I read anything? My mind worked hard, but as I tried to pull the letters and sounds from my memory, there was nothing there but screaming silence. My head began to feel dizzy. It throbbed. I was enmeshed in a swarm of fragmented thoughts that jangled inside my head. And when I wanted to pull one complete idea out, it got snagged in the mess. I didn't have a way to yank it out. My tools of learned grammar and semantic speech were gone.

The next day, Kathy gave me a blue-lined book. She would write items in it every day for my homework. It was similar to what my school teacher used to do. Kathy would write words in my notebook, using simple directions. Then, in front of the mirror, she would go over them with me many times to make sure I pronounced them correctly. She would repeat a word several times and then we would say it together. But, when I had to repeat it alone, I would forget what the original sound was.

Looking at my hollow mouth, I would try to remember and enunciate those sounds. But each time a garbled noise came out instead, no matter how often we practiced together. It was frightening how I had to relearn the placement of my teeth and tongue for each utterance. My dysarthria made things even worse. The paralyzed vocal muscles, mouth and tongue wouldn't move the way I wanted them to.

I must have spoken each word 500 times a day to my mother, a neighbor, or anyone else who was willing to listen to me. The first day's words were "Yes" and "No." The second day's were the numbers one to ten. Next were the days of the week. Then we got to words beginning with vowel sounds: "up", "eat," and "out." We progressed to common nouns, starting with household items, parts of the body, and then members of a family. Later, we moved on to consonant blends, with "sl" and "bl," and to word associations: "bread and butter," "knife and fork." Eventually we did some into spelling: k-n-i-f-e.

After two weeks, we were finally ready for simple arithmetic: how many pennies equal 50 cents? How many dimes are there in 20 cents? We looked at ads in magazines and constructed sentences to improve my language formation. Each day the items became more and more abstract. As they filled my notebook, my level of thinking and memory increased and I gained a degree of confidence in myself.

I was so proud of saying and writing those simple words. But because I had no memory of my own to enable me to talk spontaneously, they had to be words from somebody else's mouth. I was like the mythical nymph, Echo. I had no original words of my own but I could repeat the words of others, storing them in my memory bank to be used again.

This problem was highlighted when I telephoned John each night. The first two weeks at home I "talked" to him every night. There was little conversation, as I was not even able to say "Hi," or "I love you." I didn't have enough word memory to speak—or even the strength to dial his number. My mother would just hand me the phone after she had made the call and I would anxiously listen to the rings, waiting for his voice. I would get on the phone with my fragmented thoughts and confused emotions, and pour out some mixed-up sounds. But all the calls ended abruptly. There were no words coming out of my mouth and he was too shy or too uncomfortable to speak. In the past I was the bold one and always did the talking. Now this had to be reversed.

I needed Kathy to fill me up with words. I had to deny the fact that there was more to speech than repetition. I relied very much on Kathy to give me back my language, and I believed she was the only one who could do it. Somehow we would find it together. All

I had to do was repeat what she said and I could talk. With more hard work I would be talking like my old self again in a matter of a few months. Of course I was denying the creative and spontaneous aspects of speech that make proper communication possible.

But that changed. By the beginning of July, I was no longer able to hide from the truth. I had extreme difficulty verbalizing phrases. Now I had to work consciously through a very detailed process of mental gymnastics just to speak. At the first level of this process I had to choose the sensory stimulus, such as taste, touch, sight or smell. But I had lost that ability and now I experienced all the senses going on inside my head at the same time. Amidst all this confusion, I had to form ideas and find their proper sequencing. Once I got through that, my broken mind had to search for phrases and put order to them. Finally, I had to find each precise word, with its correct intonation. I felt I was in the midst of a cyclone with my brains tossed all about.

What made this even more chaotic was having to remember every prior level in order to go on to the next one. This was all before I could utter one simple statement of my own. No wonder my speech came out so snarled and error-ridden.

My aphasia was more than a physical problem. It involved my whole social and emotional being. With the exception of John and my family, I had no one to connect with who remembered the old me. Society chose not to understand me any longer, and was too impatient to even try. I had to tolerate constant interruptions, and people not understanding what I was saying, or just ignoring me. With my past world forgotten I had to take this uncharted journey alone, redefining myself through the chaos of aphasia. There was no miraculous prescription drug for me to take.

CHAPTER FIVE

Disguised Blessings

Journal entry:

> Someday when all this is over
> Someday we will have a garden,
> to pick tiger lillies from,
> and acres of tall grass
> to lie there naked, holding
> eachother, like entwined wheat.
> With soft breezes making
> our bodies float.
>
>
> Someday when all this is over,
> We will look at one another,
> And were for the first time,
> will be crying & laughing
> together

What made the stroke even more tragic was not being with the
one I loved. John only drove down to Pennsylvania a few weekends that summer. When we were together, I tried to forget that I
was disabled. I wanted to prove to him that I was the same woman
he had known in college. This was a disguised blessing for me.
Though his visits attempted to shield me from the world, they put
me in touch with it, painfully exposing me to its harsh realities.

The whole month of June I impatiently waited for his first visit and filled my mind with dreams of us. Those fantasies were my only happiness, removing me from my present reality. While I was with Kathy, practicing my vowels during speech therapy, I dreamed of the time I would be able to have a conversation with him. In Teresa's room, while I was making a wallet, struggling to pull the stitches tight, I fantasized about changing our baby. And at home each week, I would bake him chocolate chip cookies, with my mother's help in preparing them for mailing. The hardest part was spending an hour writing a legible address label with all of the spelling correct so the postman could read it. But I did all these things with love, so no matter how long it took, I persevered.

John was my primary motivation and I was determined to improve my body and mind for the sake of our relationship. He was the incentive I needed so desperately, my knight in shining armor. All I knew was that I had to be with him. But his work as a veterinarian assistant involved putting in extra hours on Friday nights and Monday mornings; he had to make sure that all the animals were bathed, housed and fed. However, he would finally be able to take time off on the Fourth of July weekend. Everybody would be celebrating the country's independence—would this be mine as well? Getting out from my parents' home and medical institutions signified my freedom.

The last time I had seen him was at the hospital in Elmira, which seemed so long ago. Much had happened since then, and I wanted to surprise him with the progress I had made. I needed to show him I would be brand new in the fall. And I was sure that by September I would be back living with John and teaching in Ithaca. So what if I still couldn't speak as I used to and still had trouble using my hand? I had more than two months to recover; that would be more than enough time. Now the old me was being tested with what she could do.

I was a model patient, positive and optimistic. I was sure there was a way for me to straighten out all these damaged parts of mine. I would just have to work as hard as I could, every minute of every hour, until all of me was there. It wasn't the time to think troubling thoughts, but instead to think romantically of my weekend with John.

Feeling nervous but exuberant, it took five hours of preparation to just look like myself again, before the stroke. I wondered as I peered into the bathroom mirror. "How am I going to transform the beast back into the beauty?"

I had regained some movement in my right leg, so my limp was not so obvious. And I did not have to wear my arm sling all the time. That was a start. But dressing was still difficult. I owed it to John and myself at least to try and tackle it.

I took a second look in the mirror and thought of the Wicked Witch saying, "Mirror, mirror on the wall, who is the fairest of them all?" I looked awful. Convinced that anything would be an improvement, I got out my make-up bag and repeatedly removed and reapplied rouge, lipstick and mascara. The first four or five attempts made me look like a circus clown, with make-up and cold cream slapped all over my face. I was getting desperate, but by the second hour the results finally improved. The old me was very slowly taking form in the mirror.

Getting dressed involved so many decisions that I was exhausted before I really began. I finally picked out a pretty pastel-flowered dress that molded my figure. It had no zippers or buttons, making it easy to put on. At least I would be my old self on the outside, which would give me confidence. But what about the inside? How long would this pretty past image of me last, before I drooled. Or, like Cinderella, could I run home before my true identity was revealed?

These thoughts vanished when the doorbell rang at 10.30 pm. John was here! I was at the top of the stairs, so my mother answered it. He came in, looked up at me and smiled. His grin confirmed how well the many hours of preparation had worked. I wanted to say that I had missed him terribly, but the words wouldn't come. That didn't matter because John was here now and could be my protector! All those awful feelings were banished by his presence and smile. Hanging on to the banister, I made my way down to his arms, and he swooped me up in a warm hug. Holding on to him tighter, I was afraid to let go. It was so exciting, finally having him here. Nothing else mattered. At that moment all my pain and anguish vanished. But I was also so tired from the hours of anticipation and preparation that I could easily have fallen asleep right in front of him.

I needed some sort of magic potion to keep me awake. I didn't want to become a Sleeping Beauty for him. I had envisioned our first time together as very passionate. Instead, I was falling asleep at the bottom of the staircase. Although he had just arrived, I couldn't help constantly yawning. That destroyed any chance of romance. Like a little kid, I had to excuse myself and go upstairs to bed while he unpacked his things downstairs.

The next morning, while he was still sleeping, my mother helped me surprise him. I made his breakfast, preparing bacon, toast and eggs. I would never have tried this for anyone except him so soon after my stroke. The cooking was really difficult, but I felt such happiness when I served it to him. Even though I was unable to use both hands in the preparation and cooking, I was learning that one hand is certainly better than none. But I still had to learn patience, because my timing and judgment were so incredibly off.

I didn't have anything ready on time, as I used to. And now, the sunny-side-up eggs came out scrambled and the toast and bacon were burnt! It seemed I worked a lot harder and created more of a mess. The pots and dishes were all over the place and caked with grease. Despite this it must have smelled good, because he came into the kitchen smiling. As he ate hungrily, I just watched in amazement. How could he think this cooking was good? I was convinced that the next time would be better, but Julia Child I was not.

After breakfast we decided to take a drive in the country. This was my first ride outside of therapy appointments. It was a hot, humid day, and we cooled off by riding into the shady mountains. There was no tension, no third party around, just the two of us for the first time, alone together. I felt so good just sitting next to the man I loved as we held hands—his right in my left. It was perfect that our hands matched that way, where I could feel his warm touch.

We came to a beautiful field with pine trees bordered by tiger lilies. We both knew this was the place to be. Getting out of the car I felt a freeing sense of sexuality that did not belong to disability.

For a while I was free from my struggles as we melted into one another on the soft ground. I was reminded that I was still a woman who deeply loved a man, and even disability couldn't take that away. By the time we returned to the car the earth was all shadowed and cool. Everything seemed so serene that I felt like I was floating. As we drove in wonderful silence I felt warm and secure, so distant from my weekday turmoil.

We decided that we felt so good together, we should be daring and go dancing that night. We pictured it to be like old times back in Ithaca. Before my stroke I used to go out dancing every chance I could get. When the music started, people smiled at me with admiring glances. I loved the way music put magic in my body and I would become one with it, a mindless, primitive pleasure.

For at least two weeks I had secretly practiced alone in my parents' basement. I wasn't using the cane any more, and I thought I was ready to show John what moves I could still make. Putting some lively music on, I made sure no one else could hear and, tapping my left foot, I danced across the carpeted floor. Could it be that I moved differently now? Shaken by having two left feet, I was nevertheless convinced that I had not lost the one talent that made me feel so alive. Maybe it was that I didn't have a partner or that my feet stuck to the carpet.

That night at the disco, sitting down, tapping my foot, I swayed my body to the beat of the music. Slow dancing was going to be really romantic and make my heart race. But I was excited as I waited for my moment as the music livened. I would face John with sensuality and dance on my own.

I was ready and could not wait any longer. I motioned to John that I wanted to start. Leaping onto the dance floor, however, I found that my feet didn't move with the music. Something was terribly wrong. I had the mental image of my body floating in graceful motion but instead, my feet felt as though they were cast in cement. They were stuck, while the rest of me flapped around like a fish out of water.

I couldn't comprehend what had happened or what to do next. I just stood there feeling ashamed, with everyone staring at me. Then, taking my arm John gently took me back to our seats and collected our coats, and I lagged behind him to the exit. There was a heavy silence all the way home. When we got back my mother met us at the door, anxious to know why we had returned so soon. Too upset to tell her in my disrupted voice, I rushed to my bedroom, leaving John to explain.

I awoke the next day with a terrible headache, knowing all too well that it was John's last day with me. I didn't know when I would see him again. But I couldn't have him go away with last night's image of me. Convinced I was going to cheer us up, I walked down to the basement to wake him with a kiss. He was still asleep, looking like a little boy with his eyes closed and hair all tossed. I thought of yesterday and how we had hugged and kissed in that beautiful field. I wanted to feel that again. As I leaned down to put my lips on his cheek, I noticed something out of the corner of my eye. The suitcases he had brought back were open, spilling out the summer clothes I had planned to wear for him in Ithaca. Little did I know that my mother had talked with him earlier that week, telling him to bring my clothes to Altoona since she did not know when I would be returning.

The drumming in my head got worse. Stunned and unable to catch my breath, it was as though someone had pushed me down a flight of stairs. My feet faltered as I fell down into a labyrinth of confusion. I was like Alice in Wonderland falling between two worlds. Was I in Ithaca with John, or at my parents' house? The truth hit hard: at my parents' home. My cardboard house of dreams came tumbling down as I collided with reality. I had only my tears. No words could describe my feelings at losing the home I could have had with John.

That morning John drove back to Ithaca troubled about my tears, not knowing what was wrong or how to make the pain go away.

CHAPTER SIX

The Girl Who Had Everything

Dear Barbara,

I'm writing to you, hoping with all my heart that this letter will allow you to talk with me and not shut me out.

I know how you are feeling. You had to give up so much and have had so many shocking upsets. You are not feeling like Barbara Newborn, and you think that you have to hold on to John and Ithaca and all they stood for. Believe me, my darling, I do know how you are thinking and feeling. It is all part of recovering. You are Barbara Newborn. That has not changed. Your emotions are feelings within you which have been disrupted and clouded. They are healing, sweetheart. You will feel like you again. I guess we're all impatient, but now it is time to think of the wonderful progress you've made in such a short period. Know this, for it is the truth: it will be good again. But your belief in that knowing will take patience.

Dad knows you are wonderful and he is so proud of you. He loves you. So understand your father; you are his daughter. After all, he has lived 32 years longer and knows a good deal about loss, so he has to tell you what he thinks. That is why it is hard for him to control his feelings. He is not fighting with you. He is fighting for you.

You are going through so many emotions. Now you are feeling lost and without direction. But that direction, my darling, is up and up and up. And you will no longer feel lost. You will have the reins of your life again and all will be beautiful. Just remember this, when again and again you will be searching for Barbara Newborn. She is here, right here. Only you can experience the doubts but they will pass! Give yourself this knowledge. Take it and hold on to it. It is the truth. There is only one Barbara Newborn, and that is you.

Your Mom

Most of my life, I was known as the "girl who had everything." I could always smile and change costumes as naturally as a chameleon. I could be a tomboy and play with the boys and by sundown cook a gourmet meal and turn into a passionate romantic. Treasuring my life, I thought it would always remain the same earthy, sensuous adventure.

Love, independence and fearlessness were three qualities I was brought up with. From the day I was born I always felt wonderfully secure, protected and loved by both parents. Coming over to my parents' house on weekends, grandparents, aunts, uncles and cousins would give me their constant adoration and attention, being the youngest of all my relatives' children. I was a fairy princess in a wonderland where love was always there. I never had to search for it.

My fierce independence revealed itself as early as my third birthday. My mother and I walked hand in hand into our yard towards the guests at my party. I suddenly yanked my hand out, shouting to the world, "I can walk by myself!" She let me walk alone, but I knew she was lingering behind. And when I went to the beach with my mother, I would laugh at the waves, wanting to go into the ocean. Running in front of her, I would splash the waves and enter the water fearlessly. But she was watching closely, pulling me in whenever I got too bold. I always loved and laughed with the enthusiasm and passion of that fearless three-year-old, but I was protected by her love, innocent of life's threats. My mother called me her naive, sophisticated daughter.

My father also gave me safety, but allowed me independence. I trusted his wisdom and protective guidance. When I was born, he sat at my mother's side and exclaimed, "What a beautiful baby girl we have!"

Powerful and gentle, his tender care always made me feel special and unique. He often said to me while I was growing up, "You are me; you are so much like me."

Believing this gave me strength. Through both my parents I perceived that all things were possible.

But my child's world also had its complicated side. When I was growing up, I saw and experienced things that didn't make much sense. In elementary school I would wonder why everybody didn't like different kinds of people, or why kids are mean to those who are different. The popular kids seemed to be the meanest and most fickle. My friends were always a mixed group of people, and included some of the more unpopular. It wasn't that I felt sorry for them, but that they were so much friendlier and easier to know. They were all so lonely and loyal.

Linda was my friend in elementary school. We were in the sixth grade together. She was beautiful, with her blonde hair, blue eyes and soft, rosy skin. We had so much fun playing with each other. Then one day she was playing alone with matches, and there was a terrible accident; she set herself on fire. She was burned over 90 percent of her body. While she was in intensive care at the hospital she got hundreds of stuffed animals, flowers and cards from everyone. But then, about a month later, when she was ready to come home, the kids who lived on her street made fun of her appearance. Even her classmates ran away from her like the plague. I suppose they were scared and their fears made them mean and not understand. But why did they have to run away from her like that, when she needed them the most?

In the same school a boy named Charley had scaly and bumpy skin all over his upper body. What made the teasing worse was that he would grin and hug himself whenever another child passed, making fun of him. Then there were just the unpopular children who were too fat, thin or shy. They were the ones who most needed smiles from the other children; instead they were taunted and laughed at.

I suppose that parents taught their children to fear anyone or anything that was different; they dared not question the underlying truths. Linda and Charley needed friends and compassion then more than at any time in their lives. Instead, people only saw their external scars and reacted by ostracizing them. They refused to acknowledge the vulnerability felt by those affected by disease, disaster and difference. In their refusal, they prejudged people who were not as "normal" as they were.

During my high school years my family relocated three times. I lived in communities from industrial to agricultural and from affluent to depressed. In each of these environments, people had completely different social attitudes. While growing up I constantly had to adapt and adjust to those lifestyles. But this was made easier because I always knew who I was; I didn't feel threatened. It was natural for me to be involved and compassionate with people and at the same time to do my own thing. I felt part of the whole environment.

While growing up I discovered that I was sensitive to differences in each individual. I could connect with anyone and really listen to his or her views—from a corporate VIP to a country farmer. I grew up with feelings of harmony and respect for others. Regardless of their diverse lifestyles, we all had the same feelings and spirit inside.

At 21 years of age, I found myself adapting and adjusting again in my parents' home. But this time I was fearful and depressed. I found myself despising my dependence on my parents. Like Linda, my school friend, I was made different against my will. Before my stroke I had never been in any permanently damaging situation and had never been depressed for more than a couple of hours; I did not know what depression was. If I was sad because of a break-up with a college boyfriend, I would always seek the comfort of my friends. Now, however, I didn't have any friends. Because of my stroke I had lost my connections with everyone and I did not know who I was.

I was constantly struggling between two opposing mental states. One was my fear, the other my courage. The stroke had emptied me of my own identity; I became a part of whatever environment I was in. As an outpatient, when I was active and improving, I felt courageous and strong. But at home, when I was lonely and bored, I felt afraid. Then I had time to have bad thoughts. I didn't smile very often; instead, I was constantly frustrated by how to dress, eat and talk. When the monotony and the fears took over, my mother and I were often driven to tears of anguish. On several occasions I argued with her, shutting her out. I was unable to face her. Not knowing how to reach me, she only wanted me to believe in myself again. With my emotions welling up inside, and the pressure rising in my head, I was caught in a trap. Trying to escape the tortures of my mind I would dash out of the house, slamming the front door behind me. Once outside, as I looked around at the distant mountains while breathing in the fresh air, I would feel some freedom and peace.

I would return home after at least an hour of being outdoors. Then, walking upstairs to my bedroom, I could write of my chaotic fears, attempting to make sense of the crazy, mixed-up world I was now in. There was so much I didn't understand, but intuitively I knew that recovery meant living through these uncertainties. No matter how disabled my language, I had to hear my inner voice to remind me who I was. Even though I was constantly blocked by my bad grammar and spelling, I had to write down my feelings. The only person I could really talk to was myself; there was no one to interrupt my self-expression.

At the beginning of my writing, I clutched the pen very intensely because I had to use my slow and unpracticed left hand. But it didn't take long before the ideas formed in my mind. I completely forgot about time as I conveyed my thoughts directly to paper in a totally unconscious state. I was able to think more clearly and could write myself out of the darkness. Whenever I got into a black mood, I would stop it from the very beginning, like putting my finger in the dike before the floods overwhelmed me. I convinced myself that things weren't as bad as they seemed. If I had experienced these emotions fully, they could have pushed me over the edge. But facing myself in isolation, my writing became a safety net, giving me spiritual strength. I searched for the remaining hope that I was still alive and thus able to dream. My writing kept me sane.

Although it must have been hard for them to see me struggle every day, my parents did not try to do everything for me. They understood that I needed more than anything else to feel capable, and treated me as normally as possible. No matter if it was slowly tying my shoes or stumbling through a sentence, my independence put quality back in my life. And I was able to remind myself who I was, a little at a time. While others were uncomfortable seeing me as helpless, my parents knew I had to endure the challenge. My family dared not treat me like a baby, but as their intelligent and independent daughter. They knew who I was even though I had forgotten, allowing me the dignity of reconnecting with myself.

I took on full responsibility, not for my sickness but for my health. I tried with all my being, everything I knew, to get well again, to take the necessary risks to recover. I had always taken risks in the past, and this present situation demanded the same of me. If I accepted excuses or blame for my sickness, I would not get better, and that would mean that I was not doing all I could. Excuses would only make me stay where I was and not go on, no matter how tough it was. I could not add these negative emotions to my already confused spirit. Yes, I was struggling, but I was not blaming, especially not myself. If I had done that, I would have remained frozen. A common reaction to tragic situations is to blame someone or something for causing it to happen. The illusion of a wrathful God punishing us for our sins gives us someone to blame, thereby reinforcing our feelings of being a victim. We are then caught in guilt.

With my family's support, no matter how dismal the days seemed, I knew tomorrow would be better. We were immersed in healing. But how could I progress at home without a therapist? Refusing to give up, my parents and I invented games out of our own ingenuity and desperation. We used these home-made remedies even on long car rides. My mother, holding a dictionary, thumbing through the pages, would test me on the spellings and definitions of words. And when we were tired of doing that, we would think up funny tongue twisters and I would repeat them through the course of the drive.

A game I enjoyed playing with my father was to call out the names on street signs. But sometimes he was driving too fast and my mind was too slow to read them fully; the signs would blur past. However, he kept me in good spirits because we silently shared a bond that put me in touch with a very safe and warm place.

A really important occasion was when my parents took me to an educational toy store. I enjoyed walking through the aisles, picking out several toys designed to develop children's mental and physical abilities. But I planned to use them to build up my own skills. I was excited to get these new games home because relearning language had been the most challenging feat for me yet. I could live with a feeble walk or a paralyzed limb, but it was hard for me to exist for the rest of my life without communication. How does one learn to speak, read, write and listen with brain damage?

The first few weeks after the stroke I practiced the alphabet each day but had trouble remembering the letters. When I tried writing words that began with each letter, my memory was so poor I had to rely on the alphabetized listings in telephone books or the dictionary for help. I had to use lined paper because I could not write with stability, and many of the letters I tried seemed backwards, upside down or in a foreign alphabet. Switching hands caused my printing to be sloppy and slow, worse than a child starting school. It was very different from my teacher's handwriting, which was very smooth and neat, with big letters.

At first I didn't even know how to hold the pen in my left hand. For about half an hour I tried all the positions, but everything seemed uncomfortable. I tried twisting my wrist, having my fingers grasp the pen in any position as if for dear life. I even turned the paper backwards, forwards, sideways, at every angle that is known to man—the complete 360-degree circle. I couldn't use fountain pens because now I was left handed the ink on the paper would smear all over my hands. When I was finished I looked like a two-year-old who had been finger painting. While trying to reteach myself to draw or paint, I thought of how many watercolors and Indian ink drawings I had done while at college. I used to create the most intricate and fine lines. Now I couldn't even draw a simple thing like a circle.

When I tried to type with only my left hand, I had trouble with the alphabet and could not remember which keys to press. I had been able to type 50 words per minute; my current rate was one word per minute, and now I became dizzy because I had to constantly select from all those keys.

To regain my reading skills I would practice spelling each day by repeating words and spelling them out in my broken head. It was all very difficult, like the game of Scrabble; sometimes I could construct words but most often I could not. When I was alone, I floundered through picture books like *Cinderella* and *Peter Pan* and wondered when I would read again as I used to. In my senior year at college as a student teacher, I loved teaching my pupils to take and devour a good novel. But here I was slower than any remedial student and way below their comprehension level. I couldn't even read comics. Looking at the pictures instead, I tried to understand what the characters were saying.

Exhausted from all these activities, I sat in front of the TV and stared. My attention span was poor and the movements on the screen barraged me all at once. And viewing a comedy show, I couldn't follow any of the humor because I couldn't remember the previous dialogue and understand the punch line. Watching soap operas depressed me; their characters had lesser problems than I. Constantly comparing my slurred speech to that of the actors, I questioned when I would be able to speak like them.

One way I measured my progress in communicating was by calling the telephone operator for assistance. I would test myself by asking for information as well as I could. At first I had difficulty, stumbling over my words, but the more I practiced, the better I became, and gradually my thoughts formed together and created speech. It was far less intimidating than having a person in front of me. There were no distractions other than the voice at the other end. And I could always hang up if necessary.

However, in everyday life there were things to intimidate me. When I dared to go outside, I found it humiliating if someone asked me for directions, or to sign my name on a credit card receipt. My childish scrawl and stuttering often embarrassed me, and others were impatient and wanted a quick signature or an answer that would not come. There was absolutely no way I could tell them what was wrong.

Every time the phone rang when my parents were not home, I would become anxious. Often, I would just let it ring. The few times I had the courage to pick it up, I couldn't remember what the message was or even write it down. If the call was from a friend, our reactions would make both of us feel uncomfortable. If a stranger telephoned, they thought I was stupid because I did not speak intelligently.

I felt petrified when the doorbell rang one evening when my parents were not around. Not knowing what to do, I waited in awkward silence. But the bell kept on ringing until I had to open the door. Three surprised strangers looked at me. Were they familiar? Could they be business associates of my parents? Having only a faint memory of who they were and no fluent speech, I dared not respond. I had no idea what they wanted, so we just stood there at the door and did nothing. The tension increased and my brain just shut off. Then, after what seemed like an eternity, they let themselves in, sat down and made what must have been small-talk. But I heard this conversation as static noise. We stared at each other for over an hour waiting for my parents to arrive.

I could never completely escape my disability, for I was always reminded of it. It seemed as if the whole world were going on with their lives but me. I sadly felt that, except for a handful of people, my journal and the telephone operator, my communication with the human race was disappearing before me.

CHAPTER SEVEN

A Shadow of Myself

Dear John,

Listen, I'm going to be harder than hell to live with and at times, I'm going to feel like giving up. I just hope you can take that. I'm going through the most depressing time in my life. I have no answers of what is to come. Please John, understand me and be patient. I look to you for faith, not to give up.

Barbara

By the end of August, despite my strongest wishes, all physical progress came to a grinding halt and I was forced into the deepest depression. But I was convinced that my former self would be recovered when John and I were permanently together. What could I really depend on now except John and our future? I thought he would be the one to support me psychologically and that he would take the place of my parents when I went back to Ithaca. John would be there to shield me and take me out of the world of illness. But was it only my dream? Because I needed him so much, I was becoming a shadow of myself. I was denying my own inner strengths. This vulnerability almost became my downfall.

The second time he visited me was in mid-July. I was able to talk a bit and my facial features had returned to symmetry to the extent that I did not have a crooked smile any longer. There was even a noticeable improvement in my body's balance. To celebrate, John and I decided we would go out on the town. The only event going on that day was a horse show, and since his dream was to be a veterinarian in the country, I thought I might as well get used to the idea of having huge animals around me all the time.

As he drove to the show, I felt secure and distant from my problems, as if the whole world was just the two of us for the time being. I had always enjoyed driving with him before the stroke. I could kiss his cheek, snuggling up next to him while he sat behind the wheel. Now seated beside him, I proudly showed him the hand exercises I had learned that week in therapy. Surprised that I had learned so much in such a short time, he looked at me with a boyish grin and said, "Hey, for being such a good student, I'd like to treat you to some ice cream. Why don't we stop along the way?"

I nodded, smiling bashfully as he drove to the mall. But when he had parked the car, he had to help me out and physically support me because I kept losing my footing on the gravel pathway. I was jolted back to an all-too-familiar reality.

Inside the building, it was noisy and closed in, and the people frightened me. I was already trying to adjust to too many things at the same time. I felt that some sort of plastic barrier, like a bubble, was separating me from other people. It was as though I was walking in a strange dream state, with all those people staring at me. In the past I had known they were staring for a better reason—then I was attractive and full of life. Now I imagined that those stares were looking inside me, believing there was nothing there. I felt choked, suffocated; I needed to get out. I wanted to go home or back to the hospital where I was safe and secure, where people were just like me or worse. They were the only ones who understood me now, I thought. Not even John could comprehend.

When we finally got through the crowds, I looked at him, hoping he could sense that I was upset. But all he did was smile and say, "What flavor do you want?"

When we reached the stables, clutching John's arm, I felt protected again. As long as he was there by my side, I would not fall. Looking around, watching the events, I unexpectedly spotted an old girlfriend. Suddenly I became embarrassed because we had not seen each other for at least a year, back when I was my old self, which seemed a lifetime ago. I couldn't remember her name, so I turned away, hoping she wouldn't see me. But I heard her call out my name. It was too late. Running over to me looking shocked, she blurted out, "Hey Barbara! It's me, Carol: I expected you would be so much worse, in a wheelchair really crippled."

I really hated that remark. There was so much she could not see. True, there were no bruises or scars on my body. The stroke's only noticeable signs were limping, an arm in a sling, and slurred speech. But couldn't she realize that the stroke had left its mark on my brain? All I could do was stare at her and attempt to talk, but my speech came out all garbled.

For the first time in my life people were made uncomfortable by my presence. And I was made uncomfortable by theirs. They showed pity, not sympathy, and pity means no hope at all. Yes, John was there, but he could not protect the inner me from the pain, whether I was with him or not. He could not shield me from the awful nightmares I was having.

In those scenes, I was always deserted. In my last one, John and I were at my neurologist's house, where his teenage children were throwing a wild party. They all knew about my stroke and left me in a corner while John joined in their fun. Then he and the others started taunting me. "You're a cripple, and you'll be that way forever!"

Yelling back at these horrible creatures, I screamed, "It's not fair! I have my whole life in front of me!"

I awoke to a soaking wet pillow; it was my reality, not just a passing nightmare.

John was coming down to Altoona to celebrate my twenty-second birthday. My mother joked with him over the phone about how much I missed him, and said she was afraid that when we saw him, he would vanish into thin air. Then she said, "We don't see enough of you."

He laughed mockingly and replied, "Well, I'm trying to make myself look fatter, but cooking for myself over the past month has made me thin enough to disappear."

My mom, and I smiled at each other and after hanging up, I began planning for our glorious weekend together. We would go to a beautiful state park nearby and camp overnight, making love under the stars. And the days would be spent in pure enjoyment, having fun in the paddleboats and sunning ourselves on the beach. It would be just the two of us, away from Altoona, the hospital and the pain. Preparing for this adventure, I made all the foods he loved to eat and packed them in a huge picnic basket. I would show him what a great wife I could be.

Feeling good when we got to the park, I giggled as he helped me out of his car. The awkwardness I had felt just two weeks ago seemed to have disappeared. But as I stood up in the fresh air, a dark green bus pulled up alongside us and unloaded what looked like men-boys. They were all wearing black tank bathing suits with matching shirts, and their ageless faces had a void expression. This seemed funny to me, as I watched as a voyeur. They followed each other until they came to the water's edge, and splashing each other, they giggled. They all seemed to be enjoying themselves amidst the frenzy of laughter.

But why was I staring like this, the way others stared at me? Crashing in my head was the sick feeling that people saw me as I saw them. I wondered, "Do strangers think I am retarded just because I have trouble with my speech?"

But did I feel retarded at times? Maybe I did, maybe I didn't. How was I to know, not having a connection with anything? The only comparison I had was between my past life and now. Was it a curse or a blessing? If this was a curse, then I would give up hope and see it as the destruction of who I was through the loss of my 21 years of growth. If it was a blessing, I would use my pain and use it well. But how could I ever get society to believe I was not retarded, as I appeared to be? I was much worse than those retarded people; at least they had friends and did not know any better.

The disastrous weekend ended early. On the way home, I sat in the car pondering how I was ever going to get myself back from so many losses. Pleadingly, I looked at John, but he averted his eyes, looking down and saying, "No one will like you if you are so depressed."

Did I have to put on a happy face for everybody, including him?

John left the next day without even a good-bye kiss, excusing himself by saying he was too tired and had a long drive back. He promised to telephone me after supper the following day, but the call never came. When the phone rang, I picked it up thinking it was John, only to overhear my mother's conversation with the principal of the school where I was going to teach that fall.

"Yes," she kept on saying in resignation. Yes, she knew I wouldn't be ready this fall. Yes, I was a special person. Yes, she knew how sorry he felt about this. But there was nothing anyone could do. Yes, she had guessed the school would have to look for another teacher for my classes. A substitute? The very idea made me gasp.

Thanking him, my mother quietly hung up the phone. She would tell me about the conversation later in her own gentle way. How could they make this decision without informing me? Didn't I count? I felt such anguish at that moment that I ran out of the house as far as I could, until I came to an old hiding place in the woods where no one would ever find me. Exhausted, I dropped to the ground; the hard dirt was damp. Here no one would discover my tears.

John telephoned late the next week, promising to see me the following weekend. The last time I had seen him was when he came for that doomsday weekend in late August. This time we decided to go to a baseball game in Pittsburgh where we would have fun and did not have to face or talk to one another. But it was rained out, so we had a dismal dinner at the clubhouse instead. I was so embarrassed when my steak arrived and he had to stand up and cut it for me. I felt helpless, like a baby. By the end of the meal I was feeling awful.

To cheer me up, John suggested we go to a nearby cinema where a film called *The Scarecrow* was playing. That was the wrong movie for me to see. It was about a man who had had one too many brutal experiences from everyone and turned catatonic. No one understood him, so his mind just turned off, and he lay down and remained motionless like a corpse. During our drive home I kept on identifying with that character; I feared what too many hard knocks could do to me. Depressed and silent I felt a distance between us again.

Things had changed. After John had left on Sunday and went

back up to Ithaca I felt confused, I felt betrayed, as if we had both shifted into two separate worlds. I wondered whether we could live together as we had planned. If we did not have the same dreams, what was I going to do? Was my protector gone?

Then John finally called on Tuesday. His voice at the other end still charmed me and made my knees turn to jelly, until he said that he could not come up next weekend because he had to work the usual long hours; it was a familiar excuse. Hiding my disappointment, I stuttered, "It's just fine because my friend Bob from college is planning to stop by and see me on his way to California. I'm really excited about seeing him. I haven't seen any of my friends from school since my stroke."

John answered menacingly, "Well that's OK. Have a great time with your friend. Maybe you could go dancing with him."

A few minutes later, he called again. I was surprised to hear from him so soon.

Jealously he threatened, "If you go out with that guy our relationship is over!"

Hearing the commotion from upstairs, my mom picked up the extension and asked, "Is everything OK, John?"

"No it isn't," John hollered and hung up.

Shocked that John either didn't trust me or was more concerned about himself than my recovery, I took the engagement ring off. My whole image of him crumbled when he made that threat. I was now going to have to recover alone, with no one and nothing to help me.

All my plans were falling apart. It would all have been coming together if the stroke hadn't happened. And now that I had memory again it also triggered in me the emotional highs and lows of joyful expectations and tearful disappointments. All week I cried for my lost dreams. Life had become an unknown which I feared more than anything. I was desperate to rebuild my life, but how was I to do it alone?

CHAPTER EIGHT

Metamorphosis

Journal entry:

> *This morning I woke up feeling down. It all started yesterday, when Dr Petersen asked how I was feeling lately. I told him I was depressed at times. So he gave me his little speech, which depressed me even more. He told me I would never be as coordinated or as strong as I used to be. I can already see it in my dancing, which is one ability I hated to lose. He also said that I would have to wait an entire year before I could be evaluated on my speech (in order to see what I couldn't get back). His truth meant I wouldn't be normal, even to myself, again. This is the hardest thing I have to face.*

At first I accepted everything I was told about my disability. My self-perception was influenced by the perceptions of other people; I was at my most vulnerable. When some professionals told me, "You can never again. . .", I didn't know what to believe, especially when I saw my own physical progress slowing down. I constantly asked, "What about me? Is this the way my life is going to be, for ever?" I felt as if the world were going on without me. People treated me differently; they were too busy to remember who I was. It was as if I had never existed before.

A tragic experience often comes without warning and the patient is forced into a total dependence on the knowledge and guidance of health professionals. Too often, therapies and negative concepts are forced on a patient, demanding that he or she conform and accept. Their well-intended messages are often filled with limitations and permanent losses in a world of "cannots."

61

Such a situation may create the false impression of a patient being helpless and unproductive. And because of the intense insecurity, he or she has no defenses against the judgments of others.

For my own survival, I needed to find some truth other than what had been dictated to me. I needed to keep hope alive at any cost; it was too much a part of my spirit. What was right for me was to avoid accepting myself as a statistic in someone's research. How can we incorporate hard data into a compassionate appraisal of someone's life, and how does a professional keep hope alive, especially when things are not going well? As in all therapy the patient must ultimately take responsibility for her wellness. But it becomes necessary for the caregiver to radiate compassion, sincerity, enthusiasm and humor. The professional must be supportive while being honest, and know how to tell the facts. A delicate interaction is necessary; making the unbearable bearable is an art.

My occupational therapist, Teresa, was someone I could rely on for encouragement. As she patiently listened to my labored speech, she would often say, "You have such great spirit. A person only has to look at you to feel your courage because you smile so often." I needed even more of that encouragement after my break-up with John.

To help cope with all the fearful frustrations, something inside Teresa and I would give way and we would just become silly about the desperate situation. We would look at each other's serious expressions as Teresa adjusted my body like a mannequin. Then, after all her efforts, I would collapse. We would laugh until streams of tears poured down our cheeks. That comic relief broke the tension of the monotonous routine. It was the best medicine to neutralize the harshness of a hospital setting. As long as I had people like Teresa to believe in me, I was able to persevere.

During the summer months my right arm, still in a sling, didn't have any range of movement. It would take a miracle to move it on its own. Try as we might, no matter how hard we worked, we still could not make any progress. Then one day Teresa directed me to move my arm to some talcum powder she had poured on the table.

"Do you really think we can make it work this time?" I gasped.

Without a moment's hesitation, she released my arm from its

sling; it slumped down at my side, looking lopsided like the rest of me. Sitting me down, she placed my arm on the table, 2 inches away from the powder. "Are you ready?" she whispered in excitement. "I'm going to do a magic act, putting a spell on your arm, telling it to move on its own to the powder. Abracadabra!"

After several attempts, I tried to move it by sheer will but still it would not budge. My body filled with tension, so I shut my eyes and concentrated one more time. It was then that I mentally entered my own arm, totally unaware of anything else in that room. Putting myself in a meditative state, I totally focused on an electric current running through my arm. A minute or more passed as my mind connected with my arm's energy. Like on a ouija board, jerking and shaking, my arm finally moved.

Two weeks later, on one of those hot, sticky summer nights, another extraordinary thing happened. Teresa and I were doing an exercise together with a 5lb weight wrapped around my right wrist. She helped me at first by lifting my wrist for me, then, after many times, she gave me a chance to do it on my own. But it was late and when she saw I had no strength left, she said "Let's try again, tomorrow."

She was just about to remove the weights when I shut my eyes tightly and focused intensely as before. Again I felt that electrical connection and my wrist turned itself over, weights and all! Smiling through my tears, I realized that this opened up so many possibilities for me. Now I would be able to move my right arm and hand in new ways. I was beginning to feel a new sense of faith in some outside force. But this also kept alive the false belief that, physically, I would be my old self again.

One evening, after Teresa and I had finished our session, she turned to me as she put away the exercises for the night. "Barbara, you will probably always have difficulty moving your right hand. You will most likely never be able to use your fingers with any dexterity."

She was reaching out to me and telling me what she thought to be true, but her words came from her experience. I did not challenge the authority underlying her interpretation, so I gave up hope of ever being able to move my hand again.

Excusing myself, I walked upstairs to my bedroom, got undressed, and went to bed crying. This was one of the worst nights of my life. What Teresa had told me was harsh, and I was not yet ready to handle it. In bed, I was still painfully aware of Teresa's words, forced to face this horrifying verdict: I would never be able to use those fingers, they would be frozen that way forever.

Over the next week my whole world went into a complete downspin. My parents drove me to stay at my favorite aunt's house in Long Island, New York, while I went to the hospital in the city. Dr Reuben, the neurologist there, had ordered tests for me to take. In the past month my mother and I had spoken with Dr Reuben several times by phone, and his voice and words had reassured me. It seemed strange that we had lived on the same street as his family for 13 years and that I used to play with his children. Now, in this tragic drama, we met again, eight years later. It all seemed too coincidental.

After waiting an hour, I was told to go into his private office where he proceeded, like a friendly uncle, to examine me for my physical reactions. I had to walk a straight line, stick out my tongue and wave my arms.

"You're doing very well," he concluded. Then he made himself comfortable in an overstuffed chair behind his large mahogany desk, and I took my place opposite him, anticipating his words. I sat silent, with a smile, waiting for the good news. He cleared his throat and began in a dry tone, "You are doing very well, but it will take you at least two years before we can tell if you will get back your full range of speech."

I gasped. "Two years until I am able to speak again," I thought. "Two years of stumbling, like a drunk, not being able to communicate with anyone at all!"

Dr Reuben started to speak again. In no time, people will never know you had aphasia. You know, I had aphasia, once. Others couldn't tell; only I could. You didn't know what happened to me, before, did you? I was a disc jockey." He smiled proudly, and then he complicated everything even more by saying, "And you really don't need a speech therapist."

"What do you mean, I don't need one? How else am I going to get my speech back?" I thought pleadingly.

I left his office, head down and silent. All the way back to my aunt's house, I kept thinking over and over again, "These next two years were supposed to have been the best years of my life."

Maybe Dr Reuben was right. I could not rely on Kathy to be my speech pathologist any longer. I wasn't improving in my language ability. I had surpassed the basic lessons she had given me, but still could not speak with fluency.

Conservative Western medicine did not know how to help me, and I felt trapped by traditional scientific standards. They could not offer me the miracle I desired. I had measured my faith solely in terms of my physical recovery, but when that faltered, I was unprepared for the results, and had absolutely no idea what to do. My mother saw how terrified this made me and began a desperate search for a miracle worker. This devastation was somehow creating room for a completely new beginning.

It was at this point that Linda entered my life. She was the new speech pathologist my mother had found. She had bright red hair, and a gracious smile, and spoke in a very friendly manner. I liked her right away.

Linda worked with me through October and blended her work with compassion and drive, not letting me get away with anything. I had to do two to four hours of homework every day. It was just like being back in college, but this time I was not prepared. I felt I was in nursery school, and suddenly taking a huge, 15-year jump into college. Nevertheless, I looked forward to each session, when we would spend hours just getting to know each other. I finally had someone who communicated, not just by sounding words and vowels. I was completely accepted, and I came to life when I was with her. Although my world was filled with sorrow, we entered a totally new realm of intimacy which I had forgotten.

Was she a miracle worker? I don't know, but I followed her leads and we took great strides together, fighting for the same purpose. Our energy was boundless. We combined hard work, determination and belief in each other. Most important, Linda began to show me that communication does not have to depend on words, supporting my desire to be involved with people and life. She helped me connect all my feelings and thoughts with gestures as well as sound. That was the real language for us.

One night in early October, I had a profound experience. Linda invited me to go to a party with her. I was very anxious, but the minute the door opened, her friends welcomed me into their home with open arms, as though nothing was wrong with me. We all sat on the couch talking, and our conversation became so engrossing that I completely forgot about my defective speech. I forgot I was aphasic. They were truly interested in who I was and what I had to offer. I had longed for people to look beyond my disability and to see me, valuing my essence as a person and not just the words I spoke.

For the first six months, I found myself breaking apart, shifting, desperately searching for new answers. In the hospital, as I looked around me, I began to realize that faith, support and laughter might be the qualities that matter most, making life worth living again. I saw people of all ages and backgrounds helping each other. The smiling faces around me seemed remarkable. I was not the only one in the world with tragic problems. There I was surrounded by people who were just like me, apart from healthy, functioning society. Everyone there seemed to sense what pain and illness were. Some patients were helping each other, silently reinforcing the message, "You're not alone."

There were a few patients, at different levels of recovery, who did not share this attitude. They seemed desolate, lost in their own fears. But there were also those who thrived in their journey, regardless of what their suffering had been. I met three people who taught me that my spirit could become free—body, mind and soul. They would not give up on life, despite the severe batterings they had suffered. While they were physically disabled, they seemed to savor every moment and were more alive that anyone I had known before.

Ken was paralyzed from the neck down as a result of a college football injury. About a year after his accident, he continued taking courses in a mechanical wheelchair. He knew now he was going to help people in similar situations, that after graduation he would become a therapist. But these are just the physical facts. When I was with him, we would smile at each other for hours; his face was bright and warm. We would forget that we were physically disabled. Allowing our spirits to run free, we were excited by our souls' connection. Ken's purpose in living changed and his perceptions grew, giving him more reason to live than ever before. His tenacity and service to support others made his spirit persevere to find joy.

The second man was also extremely brave. Four years before I met him, Larry had been told that he was going to die in six months from Wilson's disease, a rare liver malady that affects the central nervous system. If Larry ate certain foods that contained copper, he would have no control over his limbs. Although his life was physically painful, Larry's desire to live seemed to transcend any sentence of death. He was a 6th grade schoolteacher, helping children in every way that he could, and his joyful spirit kept him alive and teaching for many years to come. He repeatedly proved that the mind, working with the soul, has a lot more power than the body.

From these experiences I began to really appreciate the concept of "mind over matter." If I accepted that I couldn't do things, I would actually be telling myself that I was unable to do them. People defeat themselves when they are too afraid to even try.

I realized that all the more when one day Jim walked in as I was working out on the treadmill in the therapy room. He had lost one leg from the knee down and was wearing a prosthesis. He told me that he was diabetic, and over the years his leg had just gone numb and turned gangrenous. Scared as he was, he had his surgeon amputate it, knowing his life was in danger without the surgery. Now he seemed self-assured, dignified. His soul shone as he looked at me and smiled. Then he got on the other treadmill with his new plastic leg, ready to work out, as though nothing had changed.

Thinking of ourselves as comrades, we admired each other's courage through our smiles and tears, reminding each other that our internal strengths could put us back in touch with the world. We were kindred spirits, questioning whether suffering has to remain a tragic experience.

I marveled how, no matter how disabled their bodies were, some people could show such optimism and compassion. I found myself looking up in awe to these three men, who reached out beyond their immediate struggles. They looked deep into their hearts for truth. I sensed that they were made stronger by their suffering. They were forced into another reality that most people would not choose. Since their bodies were not working well, they had to search in another direction, looking into their own souls to find new meaning for their existence. Thus, their journeys were altered, and they had to take a road less traveled. Their refusal to give up kept them in the fullness of their power as individuals, preventing them from spiritual defeat. They perceived their joy as a universal experience and a rising compassion opened them up to nurture others. Although there was no cure for their physical suffering and disablement, they would not allow their human spirit to be destroyed. From struggle they developed resilience and love.

I had to start with my own mindful attitude, realizing that my spirit was influencing my choice between tragedy and happiness. But I would first have to look deep into my sorrows to find new direction. Only then could I seek everlasting joy. It was completely up to me now to elevate my own quality of life. I understood that when I panicked, I was without hope because I lost contact with myself. Despite the physical destruction caused by paralysis and aphasia, I was determined more than ever that nothing should prevent my healing. I knew that the inspiration for recovery was within me. My reasons for living would come from the heart. It was the onset of my metamorphosis.

CHAPTER NINE

Newborn

Journal entry:

It hurts to relive the past. Especially if all your memories are beautiful. College—four years of fantasy living that was surrounded by protective gates. Then it seemed very real to me. It's over, now. I try as hard as I can to relive it. But it's so painful because I can't. Like all castles by the sea, the waves came roaring in, like powerful hands of foam, and destroyed it, forever.

It is the unknown of the future that makes me try and live in the past. The past welcomes me to the familiar. The foreboding future leads me helplessly into the foreign. If I knew I was going to be happy again, I'd gladly take the future. You'd think that by the way I was talking I had a choice between living in the past or the world of the future . . . Oh, don't I wish.

I'm deeply afraid of the future. Maybe that comes with the feeling that I have no control over it. One way man could try to control his future is by organization and plans, to try to put his chaotic world into some semblance of order. I can't live moment by moment, or day by day, having the unexpected cripple me. I must plan! But I don't know the right decisions to make. It's driving me crazy. I can't help thinking about the future and what I am going to be capable of, or what's going to make me the happiest. But I can't do anything about it now. I'll have to wait until I'm well.

God, give me patience, or let me see faster progress. Help!!!

That autumn, I made the choice between stagnating in Altoona and moving back to Ithaca to rebuild my life. After all, it was the place where I had experienced so much happiness during my four years of college. Ithaca reminded me of who I was before the stroke. Why was it so important for me to find my past identity? By experiencing everything again, my future was going to be carved out of my past. I needed that familiarity. My instincts told me there was no other option.

My life presented me with an ultimatum the morning I woke up and looked out of my bedroom window to see my neighbor Lynn leaving for Florida. She was taking an extended vacation to visit her boyfriend. Although it was a month since I had met her, I had grown used to spending a few afternoons each week at her house after therapy. Working so hard each day, I needed that escape. Lynn's mother would make us iced tea and we would sit around the kitchen table. But now, watching from my window, I wondered, "How will I fill my afternoons now?" Abandoned, I thought, "How could she do this to me? She is going to Florida to be happy, much happier than I."

My emotional world could only gauge things in basic contrasts, black and white. In reality, Lynn was leaving to fulfil the needs and desires of her own life. But to my eyes, she was leaving me when I needed her, and she just couldn't be replaced. At that moment I wanted to get away from all the depression and go back to the place where I had come from.

"To live in Ithaca again, with all of my friends, a social life and real normal living . . ." If this was my decision, I had somehow to convince my parents to let me go. Although I still had trouble moving my right hand and arm, natural living was my very best therapy. At the beginning of September, the hospital had released me, claiming I had completed their programs and was capable of functioning in daily life. I could dress myself, do my own housework and cook simple meals. Even my speech therapist Linda agreed with my decision, and said it was a good thing for me to live with young people again. "Having conversations with your friends in Ithaca will certainly help you progress faster."

That morning was a tearful one. When I approached my parents with the idea, I was unable to argue a point in my defense. There were very few ways to describe my feelings, and I was not equipped with words of logic to reason with, so the only way I could think of to express myself was to cry. Like a two year old, therefore, I threw a temper tantrum. My mother had never seen me behave like this, but I willfully cried tears of frustration and wouldn't budge from my bed. She had to call my father at work to come home immediately.

My father sat by the edge of my bed and, leaning over me, softly asked with tears in his eyes, "What do you want? I'll do anything that you want."

There was a moment of silence, and then I stuttered hesitantly and said, "To go back to Ithaca and live there."

My parents looked at each other in shock. They hadn't thought I was ready for that decision yet. They wanted to protect me. After all, I had just broken up with John and had also received the news that I was unable to teach. Besides, who would take me to therapy in Ithaca? And who would be there when I needed someone? But after that morning, they knew their daughter had to rediscover her vitality, and in Altoona that was impossible. They realized that in Ithaca I would have the comfort of the past, and feel at home again.

After arguing back and forth the entire month, having difficulty verbalizing my thoughts, I went to my bedroom and spent many hours composing a list of reasons why I should leave. By the time I was through, I felt like Moses trying to convince the pharaoh to let his people go.

Like my parents, I was also anxious about what I might find in Ithaca. I would be re-experiencing everything as a completely different person. So we finally agreed on my having a trial week up there before I did anything permanent. Coming to a mutual decision was a big relief for all of us.

That decision I made with my parents was the most crucial one to my healing. Perhaps it is the choices we make while still in the state of fear that make us what we are and will become. How we perceive them either brings us hope or dulls our existence. Although I knew I could not live in Altoona any longer, I was taking a risk moving back to Ithaca. My new life would start with actions based on my own free choices. If I didn't act on what I really believed, my spirit would have become dimmer. In my heart, I knew that going back would bring me joy. I would start a whole

Ithaca *Sept 30* *What about I br. Were meant + gr.*

Home

The adds

1. Where all my friends are

2. On an educational environment where I can audit classes, go to the guest lectures, see plays, etc.

3. I'll be more busy - cleaning apt. cooking meals.

4. I'll be less depressed which means I will be able to do therapeutic work at home.

5. I'll lead a more normal living situation up there.

The minos

1. *The type of therapists here.

2. My mother cooking meals

3. I don't know if I will I would be able to take me to the Hospital 5½ wk until I start driving.)

* However, what is good is therapy if I'm too depressed to do the work.

new life, in a whole new world, different than before. I would begin to see all my experiences as adventures.

By the end of September, after a month of getting ready, I took that trial week. It was exciting preparing for that trip. I tried to be as physically attractive as ever, even letting my mother polish my nails and set my hair. When I got to the airport I felt anxious, but loving my freedom, I was beginning to feel like the old me again. I felt a little odd, because this was my first flight since my stroke, and my first time alone in such a big and crowded place. However, as long as I didn't have to open my mouth or use my right hand, no one would know I was hiding anything. I simply closed my eyes when I got into my assigned seat on the plane, and fell into my dreams.

We landed in Ithaca one hour later, and I was met by my friends from college. It felt just like old times. They took me to our favorite local pub. I feared that they wouldn't treat me the same as before because I had trouble expressing myself, but I was comforted and supported by their friendship. They joked with me the way they used to. There was such a constant flow of companionship and activity that I couldn't wait to move back. And so by the end of that week, without a moment's hesitation, I signed a year's lease for a furnished studio apartment. I would move in in November.

Returning to Altoona was overwhelming after my week of freedom, and I was immediately enveloped in an atmosphere of despair. I had no friends, except for Linda, and even she was too busy working. Things had not changed here; they were stagnant, and I was painfully reminded of that everywhere I went.

I couldn't wait to leave permanently. But in order for me to live in Ithaca, I had to take my driver's test again and pass. This was no small feat; it meant I would have to memorize all the driving rules and do my best to relate them to the examiner. I wondered if I would pass, since my memory wasn't so sharp and my speech failed me. It was my first examination since the stroke, but if I failed, it would mean the end of my freedom and the end of my recovery. I studied for three weeks, day and night, to memorize those rules, and be able to pronounce them out loud to the examiner. The night before the test, I became very anxious, and called Linda. When she answered the phone I said, "I can't do it! I'm going to fail."

She cut me off immediately, " I'm sure you'll pass. And to prove it, I'll bet you dinner for tomorrow night. I'll even go to the exam with you, and laugh when you have to pay for my lobster."

The next day Linda came over and we took my mom's car to the testing site. My knees were shaking as I got into the driver's seat. And when it came to answering the questions orally, I just drew a blank. I must have recited something from my memory, something I thought sounded like gibberish. But Linda was right: I passed the test! I felt like a 16-year-old again when I got into the car for my solo ride. This was such an unbelievable accomplishment for me. I was still intelligent and capable of achieving things I thought were unattainable.

On the first day of November, following my parents in their car, I made the five-hour drive to Ithaca. We arrived at my new apartment and immediately unpacked everything. It took us a good three to four hours and we were so tired, we all agreed that a good, relaxing meal might revive us. My father suggested that we go to Pierre's, one of our favorite bistros. Whenever they visited me when I was at school, we would always go there and have a good time.

When we arrived, we were seated at a table by the window. We looked out over a duck pond with weeping willows bordering it. It was such a serene scene. I felt at peace at last, but my mother still seemed a little anxious. My father was the one who interrupted our silence, and turning to me, jokingly said, "So what are you going to do when we leave? Go out on the town with a hot date?"

"Oh Roy, don't encourage her. She'll have enough boyfriends by the end of the year," my mother added.

We laughed and I struggled to say, "No one knows I'm in town yet. But the first thing I'm going to do when I get back to the apartment is call them."

Finally they had to say good-bye. Standing outside the apartment, both of them were still nervous about how many miles would be between us. I walked them to their car and we all kissed and hugged. And then they were gone. As I watched them drive off. I was filled with a sadness but also a terrific excitement.

This was the first time in my life that I would be living on my own and would finally have the freedom to choose my own destiny. My dreams would not be broken this time. Instead, they would be built on a firm foundation, my newly acquired wisdom integrating with my whole self. But in order for me to make the right decisions, I had to endure the risks that were necessary even though I was afraid. I had to overcome my fears by facing them. As scared as I was, there was no turning back. I was a phoenix rising from my own ashes, stronger and more resilient than before. My brave new world was waiting for me.

CHAPTER TEN

A Brave New World

Journal entry:

I don't know how I feel any more
Or even who I am. I knew who
I was—but like all things, that was
In the past—but I'm trying so
Hard to find, to learn, to reach out
And most importantly to search
From within. That's where the search
Begins and where the search ends
In me—people are so afraid to face
Themselves—to go through the
Rummage and dust—in themselves
To find themselves—I'm not—because
I'm not afraid of what I'll discover or better
Yet rediscover. So many people are
Afraid of themselves which makes them
Afraid of others—oh damn it—why!why!
With all that I see—I'll never be able
To accept that—everywhere I turn—people are hiding—cry
out—scream.

Do anything—but don't hide—because it might be too late—one
day—too late
To know you're hiding—and then it will be forgotten—forgotten
All lost—what were you like as a child—

To explore, to laugh, to be adventurous,
To have life and freedom—
Inhibition is taught, hate is taught
Distrust is taught—And I am hurt, so hurt
I bleed with pain—Whenever it happens to me.
Having still a child mind. To believe
In miracles—in people.
I am so hurt—I cry and cry.

But then when the night is over
and morning breaks with a newborn sun

I go and love again.

By November, I was living on my own. In Ithaca, I was away from my family and therapists, and away from all the reminders of sickness and hospitals. My new studio apartment was within walking distance of downtown and I plunged myself right in the middle of a scene of healthy young college people at the peak of their lives. It sounds perfect, but there was one small flaw: I had had a stroke just five months before. I immediately felt the contrast between me and the strangers in this town. All my recall buttons had been broken, and I did not have the proper instruction book to fix me.

Before my stroke, I was gifted with a logical mind, an attractive appearance and verbal persuasiveness. But those talents were destroyed. To survive now, I had to use the untapped resources I had not used since childhood: my intuition, faith and support. They guided and guarded me through everything from cooking a meal to taking a college course.

As young children we have no analytical thoughts. Relying on gut-level responses we cry when hungry and smile when cuddled. We are spontaneous, whether we are interacting with other children or playing by ourselves. But over the years, we forget the vital instincts that made us whole. Pounded by the heavy hand of the intellect, we are taught to brush aside our creativity and uniqueness. And pretty soon we forget what it is like to be our naked selves. Now I had to relearn it again. I had to use my instincts to make all my decisions that year.

When I was alone in silence in my apartment, I could begin to listen to my heart and not the negative clamor of other people's opinions and judgments. Meditation opened the door for much-needed self-nurturing. It was also a way I could deal with my loneliness. I needed those precious moments of self-restoration when I could retreat inside myself using meditative techniques. With the same brain that was so damaged, I was able to discover vast territories within my mind, a whole new world of peaceful sensations. And I did not have to struggle and perform the way I did in the world outside.

When being at home for too long got the better of me, I would call one of my friends. Their compassion was always there for me; they were of a nurturing spirit. When daily events were too hard to bear alone, or when strangers were intolerant, they would make me laugh when I least expected it. The people around me always reminded me that life is still good. My friend Sue would come to the apartment any time of the day or night if she heard sadness in my voice. Regardless of my friends' busy schedules, they always included me in their social plans and made me feel welcome. I could not have made it through without their efforts to make me feel like the girl they had known in college. Our relationship hadn't changed, it just became stronger because of my stroke.

That week, when I first arrived, Sue drove me to Ithaca College's admissions office, but I discovered that I was two months too late; the college session had begun the first week of September while I was still in Altoona. Taking one or two classes there would have been so familiar to me. It was the natural thing to do with my unending time; the courses would have filled at least three days a week. With a definite purpose and a sense of belonging again, I could have had the courage to socialize with other students on campus. I would be connected with Ithaca College again, and in such an intimate way. But now my plans disintegrated and there was nothing I could do to explain my position to the heartless woman at the admissions office. She delivered the bad news with no way of understanding of how it would affect me and my future. Looking up from her cluttered desk, she just said, "Tardiness."

The Wicked Witch of the North must have thought I was just another student with a speech impediment when she turned her back, dismissing me with that brief, icy statement. Intimidated, I stood there feeling totally blank; I had been so excited about taking classes and now this news was too much to handle.

When I returned home, all I saw was my scantily furnished apartment. In this lonely cave, I would have nothing to do. I could play all day, but with whom? I couldn't even fill my time with sports because of my poor coordination.

That night, trying to get myself to sleep, I tossed and turned instead, fearful of being locked inside my apartment for years. When the morning sun rose, despite feeling tired from not having slept, I somehow found the will to try again. Something inside kept me going. I began making lists of places to call for volunteer jobs. With the Ithaca yellow pages in front of me I started dialing social service agencies. But when someone answered the phone and heard me speak, they all said, "Sorry, we don't need you" and hung up. It was a crushing blow. Didn't they have any idea what I was saying? Of course, I didn't tell them that I had had a stroke, but they should have known better and shown some kindness. After all, they were social services agencies.

After feeling sorry for myself, these calls made me angry. Determined not to give in, I would try again. I was not going to believe the prejudices that others had about me. I was going to fight and prove they were wrong. I was not going to become another statistic. Perseverance—that was a favorite word in my vocabulary since 7 June.

I was reminded of how I had been able to speak on the phone, just last year. It was so easy and natural for me. I could sell myself just by saying something witty, intelligent and to the point. Could this really be my voice now; sloppy, slurred and slow? But I was determined not to give up. Staying this way was far worse than making a fool of myself.

My next plan was to seek help at employment agencies. However, I did not know what work I was capable of doing. Almost all jobs involve some aspect of conversation and require both hands. Even a secretary or a waitress needs two good hands for typing or clearing a table. I only had one—not even one, because my left hand was so inefficient. This idea took only two hours to dissolve. With my enthusiasm dwindling, I wondered about working as a substitute teacher. Would I even dare to try again? Why not? I plucked up the courage because I was desperate to find another purpose in this world besides mere existence.

The first week of December I entered the school where I had been a student teacher the year before. Knocking on the principal's door, I felt as anxious as a pupil waiting to be punished. A loud, rough voice said, "Come in!"

Walking in, I smiled, greeted Mr Sorrenson as boldly as I could, and introduced myself, carefully pronouncing each syllable of each word like a mechanical robot. "I'm Barbara Newborn. I worked here last year as a student teacher. But since that time, I've had a stroke. However, I would like to be given a chance to continue with the work I love. I would like to try to teach . . ." Pausing for a much needed break I continued,". . . if there is a position available."

Mr. Sorrenson listened with extreme patience and then exclaimed, "Why not?"

It was that simple. I was in.

Later that week, I received a call to teach. After hanging up, I started to worry about all the possible things that could go wrong. Would I fail at the one thing I loved? Was it right to go back so soon?

That morning, I did an extra long meditation because I needed to muster up some fortitude for the day. Then I drove to school, arriving well before my 10.00 am period. Walking into the teachers' lounge, I didn't want to listen to all the usual gossip about the kids. The teachers were the same ones as the year before. I had not taken them seriously then, but now I was too vulnerable for harsh conversation.

I was really in a mess this time. My insecurities about not having the same connection with the students made me anxious. During my two months as a student teacher the previous year, I was able to break through to the kids. Now, however, my confidence had been shaken.

By the time of my first class, I stood nervously as the room filled up with ninth graders, recognizing many of the faces, and wondered if they would remember me. After the sound of the bell, I introduced myself, stuttering. Those familiar students noticed the change in me the moment I opened my mouth. Most of the kids stared in disbelief. Some laughed. Many thought I was from another country, having an odd foreign accent. It was so embarrassing, I wanted to scream.

Then I gave them a spelling test, but I had difficulty pronouncing and spelling the words myself. Writing on the blackboard with my left hand was also a big problem. And it was impossible to keep their attention when I had trouble reading my lesson plans. Unable to shout above their voices, I couldn't even discipline them. And besides, the right words would not come to me in time.

Finally the bell rang and I left the room, horrified. This was worse than the break-up with John. Now all my delusions were shattered. If I couldn't go back to teaching, what could I do? With tears pouring down my cheeks, I got into my car and drove nowhere. Incapable of going any farther because of my tears, I turned onto a familiar old country road and pulled into the driveway of a farmhouse. There was a sign on the door: "Ithaca's Crisis Center." It was here that I had once been a counselor, helping anyone who came in for a meal. But now I couldn't just walk in and talk to a stranger. Besides, who would listen to me? I had always believed I was strong enough to work out whatever came my way. But this year had shown me it wasn't just a matter of my own strength and independence, but more in trusting someone enough to share my pain.

Isadora, one of the counselors I knew from the previous year, came out of the house. Walking to my car window, she asked, "Is anything wrong?" Then she recognized me, and said, "It's great to see you, Barbara. How was your summer?"

I got out of the car. As she put her arms around me, all I could do was hide my face in her shoulder.

She led me into the kitchen and handed me up a cup of tea,

waiting for me to speak. Being there in those warm, comfortable surroundings, with someone who cared, I just broke down and sobbed out all the sorrows I had pent up inside. I thought that if I started crying I'd never stop, but soon a soothing calm took over.

Although my stroke was a painful process, as long as I had someone to share the hurt with me, I could go through the darkness and come out on the other side. Before my illness, I had always laughed and had fun. I was lucky because I was born with a natural joy. And if I did have pain, I would cry alone and be all right in an hour or so. But now, I was grateful to have someone who cared enough to go through the suffering with me, allow me to experience the pain as well as the joy. It had to be that way because of the integral part this suffering played in putting me in touch with myself. This was my journey. Only when I gave myself permission to grieve for the loss of myself could I go on with the rest of my life. From the day of my stroke, 7 June, my former identity died to make way for a more purposeful life. The paradox was that the old me, with all its intense wants and desires, was the means for discovering my new fuller self.

CHAPTER ELEVEN

The Beginnings of Spring

Journal entry:

> *Did you ever seek a shadow from a distance far,*
> *And in your search you ask yourself of whom or what you are*
>
> *Or My Friend,*
> *Did you ever climb a mountain top and gasp at what you saw.*
> *A demigod upon your throne, a ruler of natural law.*
>
> *But mountain tops are also viewed by eyes from depths below.*
> *And shadows are so seldom found where'er you may forego.*
>
> *So gaze into my mind, My Friend*
> *And tell me what you see.*
> *For together we will find the dawn*
> *to live as One*
> *to live TO BE.*

On a cold winter morning in late January as I sat in bed staring out my window, I wondered what I was going to do today. Was it time for me to get outside and explore? Knowing that I had enough pain and loneliness, I was ready for anything to make the hurt go away. And besides, I was sick and tired of doing nothing, with no purpose to my time. All of my Ithaca College friends had their own schedules and lots of purpose.

I had heard that Cornell University was just starting their spring term, so that was the motivation to do something daring and spon-taneous. I also knew there would be excitement in the air, and I wanted to be part of that.

The moment I got out of my car at the parking lot, and saw in the distance how beautifully picturesque Cornell was, I knew that it was the right choice. The campus was filled with ivied Renaissance structures set against a bright blue sky and bare, old oak trees. Everything was covered with fresh snow. I had purposely forgotten the good feelings I had had on this campus the previous year with John. I now recalled them with bitter-sweet memories. It felt odd, being here alone. Almost at that moment, still feeling abandoned, I reminded myself that I was ready to explore, to have an adventure. Furthermore, I would not back down because of my fears and loneliness.

Walking from building to building, looking for students and classrooms full of activity, I wondered whether I dared do anything like this. I knew I couldn't take the courses for credit. But would any of the professors let me sit down and listen to a lecture, and just feel a part of this "great cathedral of learning."

I then recalled that throughout my four years at Ithaca College, I had been intimidated by Cornell. After all, it was one of the universities that I did not dare apply to in high school. I was one of those students who just felt that they had more personality than brains. But now it was a very different story. What would I have to lose? Nothing. I was desperate.

As I walked around the hallways, I felt like an awkward invader. As students greeted each other after their long winter vacation, I was envious. They hugged each other warmly, talking in loud, excited voices. I had no one to hug, and I felt my arm hanging loosely by my side. Everyone seemed to know someone else, except me. But I continued among the flurry, until I passed a big lecture hall, with a sign posted on the door: "Course: Minority Relations . . . Mondays 11 am to 2 pm."

It was just 10.45 am. As I peeked inside the room I saw students filling up the middle and front rows. But there were lots of seats still in the back. Plucking up enough courage to enter, I thought I could just slip inside, like a spy, and no one would notice—no questions asked. I would get lost in a sea of faces. Besides, minority relations was a subject I was becoming deeply interested in. I jokingly thought that since I was a minority of one it would be interesting to hear how other groups handled their situations. And what were their histories and futures like in this world?

The class started late in the morning, giving me plenty of time to do my usual two-hour preparations. I was starting to get over-excited, thinking about all the possibilities. Here I would make many new connections. Here I would meet friends of different nationalities and family backgrounds. And here I would become a student again. But unlike last year, where learning floated through my mind smoothly and comfortably, this year my slow, damaged brain would be compared to those of the best and brightest Cornell students. I would try my best to mend my tired brain, but I couldn't help but fear my difference.

As the professor introduced himself and the course, talking rapidly, I could not process all that he said. Of course I was day-dreaming and nervous, but something else was in my way. This was the first time I had had to pay attention to anything and stay focused, but I could not. My brain was like a leaky sieve. The minute anything entered it, it quickly went out somewhere again. If I only knew where all that information went! I knew it vanished; it disappeared like a magician's trick, "now you see it, now you don't." But where?

My attention was then drawn to how uncomfortable my wooden chair felt, and how the attached desk was on the right, not the left. It made me feel all the more slighted; it would make it harder than ever to write with my left hand. I was reminded now that all the doors to all the classrooms and buildings were made for right-handed people. That made it very difficult for me to open them now. Even though the doors were all labeled "push" or "pull", I had trouble understanding their meanings. Many times I mistakenly pushed instead of pulled. At that time even a door could put me on the defensive.

All in all, those little things made learning far more exhausting than ever before. The bell rang while I was still thinking about this, and about how confusing it was. It was the end of the first lecture—that sure went fast! But looking at my watch, it was only noon. The class was supposed to meet until 2.00. Well, it was all for the best, I thought. After all, I couldn't take in all that information, anyway. And I was very tired; I needed a break!

Sitting down in my self-assigned seat in the back, I waited until all the students had filed out of the room. There was still something so comforting about this huge lecture hall. It was as though I could be a part of something, but not be called upon to answer any questions. I couldn't possibly answer, anyhow, but no one would know, except me.

When I finally got out of the building my stomach felt empty. But I was also very aware of how crisp and fresh the outside air felt. I could not help but breathe it deeply in. In that dark lecture room, with its fluorescent lights, I had also forgotten how sunny the day was. As I started walking along the path to the student cafeteria, I saw an inviting wooden bench underneath a tall, knotted tree. Even though it was skeletal at that time of the year, it still seemed protective and grounded, with its strong, leaning branches and trunk. It seemed to echo its warmth.

The weather was cold but not freezing, so I sat down, leaning my back on the tree. I closed my eyes and felt the cool, calm air covering my face. I could not understand why I hadn't noticed before how simple, lovely and relieving it felt just to sit and relax. Sitting there gave me the perfect alibi to merely watch, observe and be part of the scene around me. I had been so active in my 21 years before, always so busy doing something or other, that I hadn't noticed it. No, that's not quite right. Rather, it was a matter of taking the time to notice, observe and become part of things. I was not the main actress on stage, but I was part of all this beauty that I was experiencing.

It had always been here for me. But why, oh why hadn't I noticed it until now? There is a proverb, "When you're ready, a door will open." Well, I was ready, and that door was opening to something wonderful, inside and out. I must have sat there for over an hour. I even forgot how empty my stomach was. It just felt good to close my eyes and feel the warmth of the sun on me and all around me. It felt like an awakening of some kind. Then getting up, I turned to that old tree, and put my arms around her trunk. And that day, instead of hugging someone, I hugged myself and the tree—all in one big swoop. Someone may have seen me, scratched her head, and kept on walking. But I didn't care about that. I had had more than enough of other people's negative views and opinions to last a lifetime.

As I drove home that day I was full of hope and vitality. I knew that this day was very important to me. And I would always remember and honor the source of those wonderful feelings. But I didn't deny that this year was going to be really rough. I felt scared, attending courses at Cornell with no one to help me. There was one important change about me, however. I was beginning to feel connected, again. I could feel newly formed electrical currents going up, down and in circular motion throughout my body and mind. I sensed an excitement which I hadn't felt in a long time. I had the beginnings of me again in a whole new environment.

It was the beginning of participating and being involved. It was the beginning of reaching out in a whole new way. I knew this process would not be easy, but I had already opened the door and entered my own wonderland. I was now a part of Cornell University. So what if I was only attending one or two courses, that would only take a few hours each week? It was enough for me to try and find my way back—and possibly, my way forward.

The next day early in the morning, I went back to see if another course was available. This time I would be bolder than the previous day, for I knew what I wanted. I was looking for a small discussion class, one that I could participate in, and get over my fears of speaking in front of others. And of course, I needed a class in which I could connect with other students.

I walked into the same building, knowing that all the notices about the courses were taped outside the classroom doors. That made it possible for me to do my own research. I read the signs very carefully and slowly, trying to understand all that I saw. I finally came across an interesting one. It read:

"Anthropology 101: An in-depth study to the beginnings of man.

Mondays, Wednesdays and Fridays 3–4 pm. Three credits."

It sounded perfect, I thought excitedly. So, what if I had missed the first class? I would catch the next one, tomorrow. Then all at once I felt a rush of anxiety. I wondered if the professor would let me sit in on the course. What if there were some kind of policy or prerequisite? What if I couldn't talk or speak up, and what if I choked on my words? On and on I went, with a hundred different questions. None of them had an answer, but they all had fear.

I must have stood, frozen, at the doorway for about five minutes, looking very anxious and confused. For just then an older man, entering the room, politely interrupted me and said, "Are you looking for something?" Then pausing, he added, "If you want to take my course, you missed the first class. But don't worry about that, because all I talked about was introductory material." Then shaking his head in annoyance, he said, "And the rest of the time was spent on class attendance and bureaucratic paperwork." He then looked directly at me, smiled, and said, "Of course, I usually ramble on. You might not want to take this class, after all."

The professor caught me completely off guard. I was surprised by his welcoming words and warmth. But I was also surprised by the perfect timing of this whole episode. Then I started dreading again, going back inside myself. I was afraid I was not looking intellectual or studious enough for him or the class. He just stood there, smiling this warm kind grin, and waiting for me to speak. I hesitated, scared to say the wrong sound. Finally, I opened my mouth to this intellectual giant and started to tell him my predicament; it took ten minutes.

I couldn't help but notice that while I spoke with lots of slurring, and missed words, he didn't flinch, turn away, or rudely interrupt. He seemed to be interested and listened with extreme patience. When I was finished, he merely asked if I would like to join his class. I immediately nodded my head in disbelief. He then said he would also help me with any papers, exams and the class material I did not understand. I had trouble accepting the reality of what I was hearing. Then we said our good-byes and that we'd see each other tomorrow. Although I was scared of this opportunity I could not refuse it, my instincts told me so. I did not know what this would lead to, but I had to try. And then it dawned on me. I was in! I wondered nervously what tomorrow and the next day would be like. But I was also learning to take each day as it comes. So I dismissed that petrifying thought as quickly as it occurred. If I didn't do that, my anxieties and fears would overcome the joy.

In class, over the next few weeks, I often forgot the questions or jumbled the answers. I would raise my hand and repeat the answer inside my head, like a mantra, saying it over and over again, hoping I would be picked before I forgot it or messed it up. But it always came out wrong, no matter how I tried. During that minute or so of raising my hand, I would lose the answer, or it would become tangled in my mind.

I would have to remember so much. In order to say one sentence, I would have to find and recall the right tone and pitch, the right word and the right grammatical structure. I always hoped that I wouldn't drool or choke on a word. The more rational, rote questions in class were always the hardest for me to answer; I don't know why this was. Maybe it was because, on top of everything I had to remember, there was still the sequencing of the factual material to get right. And then I would have to memorize so much that it felt as if my mind was on overload. The mental gymnastics in my head would just go haywire. On those occasions when I was picked, I would mouth garbled words and sounds, and there would always be an embarrassing silence when I had finished.

But then there were also classes of great creativity. They were really fun and full of delight. It seemed as if those sessions put me in a totally new world, where I didn't need to think about the answers; they just came to me. I would simply raise my hand and come up with an inspired answer. It was not coming from my rational brain, but from a special place, a more universal source of wisdom and guidance. When this happened, we were all amazed, and looked at each other in astonishment; this was not the embarrassing silence I had experienced before.

By the end of the first month I began to feel more confident about my intelligence. Some students even began talking to me before and after class, making me feel less afraid of saying the wrong thing. But it was hard for me, to sit through the entire session. I still did not grasp everything the professor and the students were saying. And I forgot about three-quarters of the material. I couldn't understand or write lecture notes fast enough. But several students volunteered to write them down for me, and explain them after class. I was really surprised by their kindness. One student wrote her notes using carbon paper, and would simply hand me my copy after class. Another suggested that I use a tape recorder so that I could listen to the class discussions over and over again, at my leisure. Both of these people helped me in such important ways. Each made a gesture of understanding and thoughtfulness, and both were magical factors. These students were not strangers any more; there was a warm intensity in their faces that made me want to know them better.

When I taped my first lecture, and then had the time to play it back repeatedly, it was the equalizing factor that I so needed; I was no longer separate from the other students. I could play the tape back, whether I was taking a shower, eating a meal or getting dressed. It seemed that I was going to class six hours a week, but my homework was becoming a full-time job. But hearing those lectures played over and over again, I started to remember what had been said in class.

My memory was getting better and better, although I still had to rely on written lists for everything: shopping list, things to do, and phone calls to make. This was helpful to me in organizing my mind and my day. I was learning how to adjust and become more independent. At last I was finding a way.

But when it came to writing papers, everything was a catastrophe. That was, indeed, another story. The ideas did not come as easily as they had the year before. I couldn't remember where the letters were when I used a typewriter, and struggled with just one hand. The previous year, as a senior, I would just jot some ideas down and then type the first draft, which was good enough to be a final copy. It used to take me, at most, two hours to do one assignment. Now, no one could read my handwritten papers; they were illegible, and filled with poor spelling, forgotten grammar and foggy concepts!

Now I had to rewrite papers by hand, about 10–15 times, each draft taking me about two days. It was a labor-intensive learning process and every time I was filled with exhausting confusion. I was constantly in a fog, going blank for the right words. I felt as though I was at school again and required to write my name on the black-board 200 times. But then I also thought about the day when I would write more fluently and freely. Maybe the next time it would be a little bit clearer than before. I was beginning to recover my lost abilities.

Late in March, after two months of attending classes, I found myself speaking out a lot more. I sometimes forgot the problems and spoke out anyway. The more I became involved, and the harder I worked, the more my speech improved. I was becoming less frightened of challenging risks. My thoughts weren't as jumbled as they had been and I began speaking in clearer concepts. I became quicker at the mental gymnastics required for speech, and my verbal ability expanded.

However, I was silent in my other class, which was held in a huge auditorium. I sat down in the last seat in the last aisle and listened carefully for all three hours. I was a bit uncomfortable at first, knowing that my brain received about a tenth of the material. But with my tape recorder in hand I started to feel I belonged at last.

It was as though I had endured a harsh winter, physically, psychologically and, most important, spiritually. Although life was still a struggle, I no longer needed a survivor's manual, feeling a renewed spontaneity and passion that came from loving life. Now I felt ready to take an enormous risk, and meet other students. It seemed I had found a perfect place in the Cornell Student Union. I couldn't wait to get there, and spent all my free time observing its exciting atmosphere. I could wait before and after classes, and blend in by just sitting on one of those comfortable well-cushioned but over-used chairs. I would pretend that I was preparing some homework, and a student would often walk right up to me and introduce himself approvingly. Soon we would be involved in an adventurous conversation. I say adventurous, because I was taking a risk with my defective speech. I would pray that I would not "screw it up" and totally turn them off. And many times I became even more tongue-tied than I already was with aphasia.

But each day I hoped I would meet someone to have a romantic relationship with, no matter who he was. I was lonely and missed the partnership I had had with John, and any compliment I received got my immediate attention. I could not hear often enough that I was beautiful. The broken me needed these assurances to build me up again. It was important that men would be charmed by my looks. No matter what wisdom I was gaining, I was still a 22-year-old who wanted to be pretty and popular again— maybe more so because I was trying to camouflage my insecurities. I would get dressed up, wearing high-heeled shoes that showed my slender legs, making sure that the old me compensated for the new. It was like wearing an outer layer to cover up my noticeably defective parts.

I was more at ease meeting foreign students because they didn't speak grammatically correct English and had an accent. Together we spoke slowly, with plenty of deliberation, but listened all the more carefully to each other. Soon we forgot about our defective speech, enjoying our communication. Our connection was magical; it just seemed to happen naturally. Each encounter started at a level of discomfort. But then, in no time at all, we were evolving together. It seemed that no matter what part of the world they were from, whatever we exchanged, either silently or verbally, we understood each other. People were entering my life again.

The beginnings of spring came that April, when I saw the melted snow retreat back into the ground, to be replaced by different shades of green grass and multicolored leaves on the trees. It was wonderful to unlock my apartment door and smell the outside air. I didn't know whether it was the warm refreshing spring that invited me outdoors to play, or whether I had had enough suffering for a lifetime. I and the earth were in transformative states, changing from death to life. With a newborn's enthusiasm, I was now ready to take new risks and open up my heart fully.

I couldn't wait to get outside. Dressing as quickly as my disability allowed, I called Dave, a friend from my undergraduate years. Feeling good, I blurted out over the phone, "It's so beautiful out, do you want to take a long walk through Cornell's campus?" Before he could answer, I pleaded, "I've been cooped up inside all winter long, and this is the first chance to be out without having to wear layers of clothes."

Dave met me in front of the campus bookstore in an hour. As we strolled, looking across the gorge, I made a shocking statement. It seemed to come out of nowhere, but it had been on my mind all week. "I can't talk that well and it still surprises me how I connect with so many different people."

He looked at me in total astonishment. "You know, Barbara, some people see what's underneath, they see your energy, warmth and courage."

My mouth dropped open in disbelief. All this time I had been limited by what *I* saw; after all, it had been drilled into me for so long that my speech was my outer personality. What Dave had just said was beyond words. It came from a soulful place.

"It's not who we are on the outside but it's our hearts that give us the ability to reach out to one another." Then he added gently, "You are still the same person as before, with the same goodness."

Dave's words that day sent me whirling. Cornell was such a different environment from the hospital in Altoona, where I saw patients just like me. In this highly intellectual atmosphere, where only the best from high school attended, I couldn't see my true self. I had been frozen in my own insecurity at not being as talented as they were. I really had no idea that other students could see "my goodness" because I had been blind to it myself.

Now Dave's words changed all that, and I began to realize that human nature can be distorted by people's need to categorize, and too often these judgments divide them from each other. We think we are our words, defending our arguments no matter what the cost. But nothing is further from the truth. If we were born into a world where silence prevailed, we would discover that our spiritual journey is connecting our minds with our hearts.

As I met people of different ages, nationalities and physical forms, the external differences had little effect on how we connected. In fact, these differences taught us tolerance, as we learned to share each other's worlds. It was not the words they spoke but rather the warm expressions of those friends that I remember most. Whether sharing our pain or laughter, we shared ourselves.

My love of people was with me constantly through the traumas of the stroke, inspiring and motivating me every step of the way in new and courageous directions. I found that when I opened my heart to others, I discovered my own wisdom deep within me. It had been there from the time I was born and was greater than anything I had ever known—infinite, divine and free.

Now I can laugh and sparkle as never before, for I know that everything and everyone is in me to stay. And nothing can take that away: no sickness, no death, no disability. I will always be. And what was always here will remain long after I am gone. It is the spirit which enables us to love each other, and creates the compassion that transforms us.

On my first flight to Ithaca at the age of 21, looking ahead at the rest of my life, I was secure of the future. However, on my return there, I had absolutely no idea of what the future held for me. I knew intuitively, however, that the rest of my life depended on this second journey, to realize the dynamic process I was a part of. Now I was learning again, not only with my mind but this time with my entire soul.

Epilogue

My stroke was not just a tragic experience. In life there are no good and bad experiences; what makes life good or bad is what we do during and after our experiences. As a result of my illness, I explored *me*, the insides of me, on a very intense level. This sounds complicated, but it is just the opposite. The illness gave me a focus for the first time in my life. I dropped all the things that were circumscribing my life and were not important. I obeyed my own spirit. I felt fortunate to have damaged my rational mind, because now I listened to my heart, what it was saying, and nothing else. Where my heart and soul directed me, I was there.

It is all right not to know the direction we are taking all the time, and in that confusion to lose our way. Confusion is not a bad thing. It tells us to stop and take time, when we do not know what else to do. Sometimes we may panic, out of fear, thinking we have to remain in control to make the unknowns known. We act impatiently, often making mistakes, causing more harm than good, and getting more distant from who we really are.

But if we just accept this confusion and take the time we need—not to act, think or judge too quickly, but be with ourselves; the problems will work themselves out. We have to be in our own inner space to take the time and patience to be alone. Then when we ask for help, we are in a better position to make discoveries or uncover the unknown past.

Illness shows us that there is nothing to fear but our own imagination of what the illness is and is going to be like. In other words, we enter a world of unknowns, where we do not control the switchboard any longer. I have learned to take whatever comes my way in life. It is not good or bad, just the other half of life. From my illness I have learned to become a whole human being, with a whole array of emotions, to be comfortable with my feelings, no matter if they are depression, loneliness and fear, to know that they are an important part of me and they are telling me something important. When we have learned fully what they are saying, they will be gone.

Be kind and patient with yourself and others, for you can only try your best in the present. The future will happen and unfold just as it should, with nothing to fear. Remember, time heals all wounds. Your time is in your journey. You do not stay where you are, you grow with new perceptions every day. You grow with new heart-throbs and new everything, and that is the wonder of life. Accept this wonder with all of its "sufferings," with all its joys and hardships. It is in the wonder that you will know you are safe and alive through it all. Even though at the time you may feel differently, with all sorts of crazy, mixed-up emotions, know that you are all right. Tragic as it may seem, right now for you, you will be more compassionate to others and yourself because of this experience. After all, joy and compassion are the substances of daily supply that we can not live without.

Please do not label yourself a victim. Physically and mentally I no longer see myself as one. The importance of this is that, because I no longer label myself that way, society does not label me either. I try never to evoke sympathy, warrant self-pity or embarrassment by excusing myself for the "shameful" stroke I had. Instead, I have taken on the attitude that I can do anything, anyone else can do.

My first 22 years of life were quite unlike my last 22. In fact, nothing in my earlier life even suggested the difficulties I would encounter later. I had never been ill or in a hospital since the day I was born. But I must say that stormy event defined my character, telling me who I was and who I was not. It led me to discover who I was to become. My instincts told me I had to connect with people again, and communicate in whatever ways were possible. Even though I was terrified, I realized I had to go through the struggle, in order to find my happiness again. It was, indeed, a challenging but also an exciting time. I tried to see that just communicating with one more person every day was an adventure. So I began my second life with that dominant thought.

I finished 1974 in Ithaca, going on to earn a masters degree in speech communication at Pennsylvania University. I was aphasic all through graduate school, and my thesis was on this subject. It was quite a struggle, but I had many wonderful people to help me along the way. In fact, my committee chairman's family edited and typed my paper for me.

After graduating I entered my family's business, a distribution company for publishing material. I set up my own department, selling educational books to schools and colleges in Pennsylvania. This was a real feat, because with the residual effects of aphasia, I had to speak on the phone or in person to several teachers each week. I spent three years working in this business.

The next summer, while visiting a friend in New Mexico, we magically founded a camp for teenagers with head trauma. I developed and co-directed various programs during the next five summers for these young adults. That helped me realize what I was destined for. I wanted to be of service to others in similar situations. I then entered New York University's Graduate School of Rehabilitation Counseling, and became a professional in this field.

For the past 11 years, no matter how many clients I have counseled, and regardless of their physical disabilities, we have discovered new ways of adapting, adjusting and finding a fuller self. In doing that we brought independence, fulfillment and dignity to our lives.

In my private practice, workshops, and position with the NSEI, I have had the privilege of knowing many courageous people, who despite their physical disabilities are tremendously enabled in spirit.

Having a stroke taught me that a much bigger and more brilliant universe was waiting for me to uncover it, with new meaning and purpose. The stroke's appearance was very bleak and disillusioning, but on the other side, there was an oasis waiting, where I could uncover more joy and compassion than I had ever known. The frightening unknowns of the future metamorphosed into the present laughter of adventure.

In essence, the world is a compassionate place. So be honest and kind with yourself and others. And be patient, knowing that it takes time to heal, to become whole. The healing starts when you allow it to begin.

Appendix:
Facts on Stroke and its Impact

The history of man has always shown examples of stroke, also referred to as brain attack. The ancient remains of Egyptian mummies give evidence of this. Hippocrates, the "father of Western medicine" wrote that Greeks suffered apoplexy, which describes a sudden, astonishing attack to the senses. Since his time, we have acquired a fair amount of information about what strokes are and why they occur.

Stroke is an injury to the nervous system, resulting from an interruption in the supply of blood to a portion or portions of the brain. This spontaneous event is usually due to a long process of degeneration of the body's blood vessels, which could take up to 20 years to develop. Arterial sclerosis, heredity, hypertension, heart disease, obesity and diabetes are some of the risk factors for stroke. It may also occur because of an inborn abnormality of the brain's vasculature. However, most are caused by clots that impair the blood flow, and produce localized damage.

The most common type of stroke is known as cerebral thrombosis, and occurs in 30–45 percent of all cases. It happens when a build-up of fatty deposits in the arterial wall causes an obstruction or blockage. The blood supply to the brain is either severely reduced or cut off completely.

A second type of stroke, called cerebral embolism, occurs when a blood clot forms somewhere else in the body. It then travels to the brain, and becomes lodged in one of the cerebral arteries. This happens in 20–30 percent of all strokes.

The third type of stroke results from hemorrhage directly within the brain. This is the most severe. It occurs when a blood vessel bursts and causes bleeding into the brain. Hemorrhage happens in a smaller number of stroke cases—5–15 percent—but the death rate is 80–90 percent.

A stroke shatters lives. Every five minutes someone has a stroke. It is the leading cause of severe disability, and is the third most common cause of death in the Western world. For instance, in the United States approximately three million Americans today are survivors of stroke. It is estimated that 550,000 strokes occur in the United States each year, killing more than 150,000 people. Most commonly associated with the elderly, stroke affects people over 65 in 70 percent of cases. But in recent years, more and more younger people are affected. Regardless of age, the psychological and physical damage is the same.

To society, one of the most devastating effects of stroke is the economic impact. The annual estimated cost of stroke in the United States is $30 billion. This includes $17 billion in direct (medical) costs, and $13 billion in loss of productivity. About one-third of the 500,000 people affected by stroke between the ages of 35 and 65 can no longer work because of disability.

The physical damage may be manifested as impaired sensation, paralysis, visual problems, difficulty swallowing or language production problems. The psychological and social damage cannot be measured; many times it may harm those affected even more than the physical damage.

This psycho-social impact contributes to the economic cost and to the cost in terms of quality of life. Between 30 and 50 percent of patients suffer from clinical depression at six months. About one-third of them will still have the same diagnosis at one year. Depression may hinder rehabilitation, thereby representing a larger cost to society. Since most survivors return home, depression leads to decreased social activity; 84 percent do not return to their previous vocations and social endeavors.

In the United States survivors are often discharged from the hospital and rehabilitation unit with significant disabilities, not only in mobility, but also in self-care. But they and their families often know little about stroke, either before or after discharge. It is important for all involved to know about the condition and how it will affect their lives. It is just as important to know what they can do about recovery. Further, despite the fact that numerous support organizations now offer information and help, those affected sometimes do not know of these resources.

To decrease the financial costs and improve the psycho-social impact of stroke, there is an immediate need for national and community resources to provide support as well as rehabilitation services. There is a further need to provide accurate information to everyone involved. Making survivors more independent will not only help them regain their dignity but ensure an improved quality of life as well.

Further Reading

BOOKS

Ahn, Jung, M.D. and Gary Ferguson. *Recovering from Stroke*. New York: HarperCollins, 1992.

Ancowitz, Arthur, M.D. *The Stroke Book*. New York: William Morrow & Company Inc. 1993.

Bergquist, W. H. McClean R. and Kobylinski B. A. *Stroke Survivors*. San Francisco: Jossey-Bass, 1994.

Birkett, D. Peter, M.D. *The Psychiatry of Stroke*. Washington: American Psychiatric Press, 1995.

Boone, Daniel. *An Adult Has Aphasia*. 5th ed. Austin, Texas: ProEd Publishers, 1984.

Dahlberg, Charles Clay, M.D. and Joseph Jaffe, M.D. *Stroke: A Doctor's Personal Story of His Recovery*. New York: W. W. Norton & Co, 1977.

De Mille, Agnes. *Reprieve*. Garden City, New York: Doubleday & Co, 1981.

Edelman, G. and R. Greenwood. *Jumbly Words and Rights Where Wrongs should Be: The Experience of Aphasia from the Inside*. Leicester: Far Communications, 1992.

Farrell, Barry. *Pat and Ronald*. New York: Random House, 1969.

Foley, Conn, M.D. and H. F. Pfeizer. *The Stroke Fact Book*. New York: Bantam Books, 1985.

Griffith, Valerie Eaton. *A Stroke in the Family*. New York: Delacorte Press, 1970.

Hodgkins, Eric. *Episode*. New York: Atheneum Publishers, 1967.

Hughes, Kathryn. *God Isn't Finished with Me Yet*. Nashville, Tennesee: Winston-Derel, 1990.

Josephs, Arthur. *The Invaluable Guide to Life After Stroke: An Owner's Manual.* Long Beach, California: Amadeus Press, 1992.

Knox, David. *Portrait of Aphasia.* Detroit: Wayne State University Press, 1971.

Levin, Rhoda F. *Heartmates.* Englewood Cliffs, New Jersey: Prentice-Hall, 1987.

McBride, Carmen. *Silent Victory.* Chicago: Nelson Hall, 1969.

Moss, C. S. *Recovery with Aphasia: The Aftermath of My Stroke.* Champagne, Illinois: University of Illinois Press, 1972.

National Stroke Association. *Living at Home After Your Stroke.* Englewood, Colorado: National Stroke Association, 1994.

——*The Road Ahead: A Stroke Recovery Guide.* Denver: National Stroke Association, 1986.

Neale, Patricia, with Richard DeNeut. *As I Am.* New York: Simon & Schuster, 1988.

Rose, Clifford and Rudy Capildeo. *Stroke: The Facts.* New York: Oxford University Press, 1981.

Sarton, Mary. *After the Stroke.* New York: W. W. Norton & Co., 1988.

Shinberg, Elaine Fantle. *Strokes: What Families Should Know.* Westminster, Maryland: Random House, 1990.

Smith, Genevieve Waples, R.N. *Care of the Patient with Stroke.* New York: Springer Publishing Co, 1976.

Strong, Maggie. *Mainstay.* Boston: Little, Brown & Co., 1988.

Veith, Ilza. *Can You Hear the Clapping of One Hand?* Berkeley, California: University of California Press, 1988.

Wulf, Helen. *Aphasia, My World Alone.* Detroit: Wayne State University Press, 1986.

NEWSLETTERS

Be Stroke Smart. National Stroke Association, Englewood, Colorado. Tel: (800) 787-6537.

Newsletter. National Aphasia Association, New York. Tel: (800) 922-4622.

Stroke Connection. American Heart Association, Dallas. Tel: (800) 553-6321.

A *Stroke of Luck*. American Heart Association, Dallas. Tel: (214) 373-6300.

ARTICLES

Dobkin, Bruce, M.D. "Economic Impact of Stroke". *Neurology*, February 1995 (Supplement 1): S6-S9.

Valuable Resources

There are many valuable resources for the survivor and his/her family. Following this section is a list of addresses of organizations which provide a variety of experiences and are able to help in a number of different ways. Many of the national associations act as guides not only for educational material but also where to find survivor/care-giver support groups. In addition, the more regional associations might be dedicated to psycho-social activities, vocational employment, therapy and counselling.

Beyond this, within each community there are untapped resources that serve as amazing potentials for the family and survivor. I suggest a family member phone to make an appointment with the hospital's rehabilitation centre that originally cared for the survivor. The social workers, nurses, psychologists, physiatrists and rehabilitation therapists should be able to help you in your search for what is available and refer you to services in your local neighbourhood. Also, do ask your support network of family, friends, clergy, neighbours and co-workers whether they know of any support or available help to stroke survivors. Neighbours might well be happy to volunteer their time and come over to the survivor's house—for instance, a good part of actress Patricia Neal's recovery was sustained by volunteers coming to her house and doing everything from puzzles with her to just being there as a comfort. I even know a few families that have started their own support group right in their living room!

Don't forget that it is vital that support should also be on hand for the primary care-giver. I have heard over and over again care-givers having no time for themselves. Don't feel selfish if you want a break from all this. You do enough! But you can't do it all by yourself; you need support too. This is as important for your well-being as it is for the survivor.

When you've got your referral list, pick up the phone and make a number of appointments to see both the person in charge and the place. Remember, you are interviewing them just as much as they are interviewing you. So ask the questions that are the most important to you and your loved one. Don't be too intimidated or shy to ask for help—any place and any person who is not there for you and your loved one, is not the right person or place.

Useful Addresses

AUSTRALIA

NSW

Stroke Recovery Association Inc.
2nd Floor
1 West Street
Lewisham NSW 2049
Tel: 02 560 0594
Fax: 02 560 2306

Queensland

Support, Self-Help and Social Activities for Stroke People
PO Box 426
Morningside QLD 4170
Tel: 07 3399 9461

South Australia

Stroke SA
Neurological Resource Centre
23A King William Road
Unley SA 5061
Tel: 08 357 8909

Tasmania

Stroke Club of Tasmania
10 Maritana Place
Claremont TAS 7011
Tel: 002 492 033 (Mrs Val Mason)

Victoria

Stroke Association of Victoria
PO Box 226
Geelong VIC 3220
Tel: 052 787 980 (Clare Gray)

Western Australia

Manning Stroke Club
138 Planet Street
Carlyle WA 6101
Tel: 09 361 3839 (Helen Sando)

Stroke Association ACT
12 Clarkson Street
Pearce
ACT 2607
Tel: 062 863 333 (Peter McMahon)

CANADA

Aphasia Association of Ontario
Bernie Dans (Chairperson)
c/o 53 The Links Road
North York
Ontario M2P 1T7

The Aphasia Centre–North York
Patricia Areto
Founder and Executive Director
53 The Links Road
North York
Ontario M2P 1T7
Tel: 416 226 3636
Fax: 416 226 3706

Aphasia Centre of Ottawa/Carleton
Gillian Galley (Speech-Language Pathologist)
R.R. #2
North Gower
Ontario KOA 2T0
Tel: 613 489 4131

Halton Aphasia Centre
Mrs Vera Goldring
345 Tuck Drive
Burlington
Ontario L7L 2R2
Tel: 905 681 8805

The Heart and Stroke Foundation of Ontario
474 Mount Pleasant Road—4th floor
Toronto
Ontario M45 2L9
Tel: 416 489 7100
Tel: 800 360 1557 (in Canada only)

The Heart and Stroke Foundation of Quebec
465 Rene Levesque Blvd, West—3rd floor
Montreal
Quebec H3Z 1A8
Tel: 514 871 1551
Fax: 514 871 1464

Shivananda Yoga Centers
Headquarters: Sivananda Ashram Yoga Camp
8th Avenue
Val Morin-P.Q.
JOT 2RO
Tel: 819 322 3226
Fax: 819 322 5876
E-M: isyvc_hq@ix.netcom.com

York/Durham Aphasia Center
Anne Wells (Administrator)
12184 9th Line South
Stouffville
Ontario L4A 3N6
Tel: 905 642 2053
Fax: 905 640 7944

NEW ZEALAND

Stroke Foundation of New Zealand Inc.
PO Box 2320
WELLINGTON NZ
Tel: 4 472 8099
Fax: 4 472 7019

UK & IRELAND

Action For Dysphasic Adults
1 Royal Street
London SE1 7LL
Tel: 0171 261 9572
Fax: 0171 928 9542

British Aphasiology Society
Jane Marshall (Secretary)
Department of Clinical Communication Studies
City University
Northampton Square
London EC1V 0HB
Tel: 0171 477 8000 ext: 4668

Disabled Living Foundation
Advice Services
380–384 Harrow Road
London W9 2HU
Tel: 0171 289 6111
Fax: 0171 266 2922

HANDYNET Ireland
Dympna Gilligan
Disability Resource Centre
National Rehabilitation Board
44 North Great George's Street
Dublin 1
Tel: 353 1 874 7503
Fax: 353 1 874 7490

LOGOPEDES
Irish Association of Speech and Language Therapists (IASLT)
4 Argus House
Greenmount Office Park
Harolds Cross Road
Dublin 6W
Tel: 353 1 473 0398

National Rehabilitation Hospital
Speech & Language Therapy Department
Joan Monahan or Paula Kane
Rochestown Avenue
Dun Laoghaire
Co Dublin
Tel: 353 1 285 4777
Fax: 353 1 285 1053

Royal College of Speech and Language Therapists
Sandy Bennet or Pam Evans
7 Bath Place
Rivington Street
London EC2A 3DR
Tel: 0171 613 3855
Fax: 0171 613 3854

The Stroke Association
CHSA House
Whitecross Street
London EC1 Y 8JJ.
Tel: 0171 490 7999
Fax: 0171 490 2686

UK Sivananda Yoga Vedanta Centre
51 Felsham Rd
London SW15 AZ
Tel: 0181 780 0160
Fax: 0181 780 0128
E-mail: syvc_lon@immedia.ca

Volunteer Stroke Scheme
Theo Davis
249 Crumlin Road
Dublin 12
Ireland
Tel: 353 1 455 7455
Fax: 353 1 455 7013

USA

American Occupational Therapy Association
1383 Piccard Drive
P.O. Box 1725
Rockville
MD 20849 1725
Tel: 301 948 9626

American Physical Therapy Association
1111 North Fairfax Street
Alexandria
VA 22314
Tel: 703 684 2782

American Speech-Language-Hearing Association
10801 Rockville Pike
Rockville MD 20852
Consumer Helpline—Tel: 800 638 8255

The Brain Aneurysm/AVM Center of Massachusetts General
Hospital
55 Fruit Street
VBK-710
Boston, Massachusetts 02114
Tel: 617 726 3353
Fax: 617 726 7501
E-mail buckley@helix.mgh.harvard.edu
Subarachnoid hemorrhage hotline: (800) 888-ISAH for immediate
referral of patients with SAH.

Carbrillo College Stroke Center
501 Upper Park Road
Santa Cruz, California 95065
Tel: 408 425 0622
Fax:408 425 0223

Center for Mindfulness
UMMC
Stress Reduction Clinic
UMass Medical Center
55 Lake Avenue North
Worcester, MA 01655-0267
Tel: 508 856 2656
Fax: 508 856 1977

The Mind/Body Medical Clinic
Deaconess Hospital
Division of Behavioral Medicine
1 Deaconess Road
Boston
MA 02215
Tel: 617 632 9530

National Aphasia Association
156 Fifth Avenue, Suite 707
New York 10010
Tel: 800 922 4622
E-mail: Klein@aphasia,org
Web: nttp.//www:aphasia.org

The National Rehabilitation Hospital
102 Irving Street NW
Washington, DC 20010-2949
Tel: 202 877 1000
TDD: 202 877 1450
Fax: 202 726 8512

The National Eastern Seal Society
70 East Lake Street
Chicago, Illinois 60601
Tel: 312 726 6200
TDD: 312 726 4258
Fax: 312 726 1494

The National Stroke and Quality of Life Medical
Educational Institute
(a division of:)
American Institute of Life-Threatening Illness and Loss
Columbia-Presbyterian Medical Center
630 West 168th Street
New York, 10032
Tel: 914 779 4877 (Dr Austin Kutscher)
Fax: 914 793 0813
Fax: 718 802 0180 (Barbara Newborn)

The National Stroke Association
96 Inverness Drive East Suite 1
Englewood,
Colorado 80112-5112
Tel: 303 649 9299
Fax: 303 649 1328
1 800 Strokes

Palms Springs Stroke Activity Center
2800 East Alego Road
Palm Springs
California 92268
Tel: 619 323 7676
Fax: 619 325 8026

Phoenix Rising Yoga Therapy
PO Box 819
Housatonic Massachusetts 01236
Tel: 800 288 9642

Stroke Connection/The American Heart Association National Center
7272 Greenville Avenue
Dallas, Texas 75231-4596
Tel: 800 553 6321
Fax: 214 696 5211
E-mail, strokaha@amhrt.org

Vocational Services for the Disabled
Tel: (800) 222-JOBS
There are different offices in each state for vocational and educational services for individuals with disabilities.

Wilderness Inquiry
1313 Fifth Street SE Box 84
Minneapolis
MN 55414 1546
Tel: 612 379 3858
Fax: 612 379 5972